BIBLE CRAFTS RECYCLED MATERIALS

By
Cathy Allen Falk

Illustrated by Brenda Mann

Cover by Brenda Mann

Shining Star Publications, Copyright © 1994

ISBN No. 0-86653-772-4

Standardized Subject Code TA ac

Printing No. 9876543

Shining Star
A Division of Frank Schaffer Publications, Inc.
23740 Hawthorne Boulevard
Torrance, CA 90505-5927

The purchase of this book entitles the buyer to reproduce student activity pages for classroom use only. Any other use requires written permission from Shining Star Publications.

All rights reserved. Printed in the United States of America.

Unless otherwise indicated, the New International Version of the Bible was used in preparing the activities in this book.

DEDICATION

This book is dedicated to friends in whom I see Jesus, through their ability to encourage, their willingness to share, and their capacity to love.

TABLE OF CONTENTS

To the Teacher/Parent 5

General Instructions for Decorating Recycled Items 6

Craft Ideas Using Juice Cans and Lids 7
   Nature Pendant 8
   Musical Instruments
      Jingle Can 9
      Shaker 10
      Clapper 11
      Drum 12
      Ram's Horn 13
   Stick Puppets 14
   Chariot 16
   Christmas Ornament 17
   Angel 18
   Nativity Set 19
   Empty Tomb 22
   Mini Easter Basket 23
   Award Day Medal 24
   Prayer Magnet 25
   Jesus, the Light of the World 26

Craft Ideas Using Paper Tubes 27
   Scroll—The Bible Jesus Knew 28
   Ark Animals 29
   Serpent 31
   Creation Viewer 32
   Centurion 33
   Finger Puppet 35
   Thanksgiving Napkin Rings 36
   Advent Candles 37
   Palm Branch 38
   Butterfly 39

Craft Ideas Using Paper Grocery Bags 41
   Twelve Stones 42
   Ten Commandments 43
   Stable 45
   Bible-Time Robe 46
   Crown 47
   Fish 48
   Love Banner 49
   Wind Sock 50

Shining Star Publications, Copyright © 1994

Craft Ideas Using Polystyrene Trays 51
   Eagle 52
   Jesus Called the Little Children 53
   Four Seasons Mobile 55
   Memory Verse Frame 57
   Love Plaque 58
   Thanksgiving Wall Hanging 59
   Star of David 60

Craft Ideas Using Cardboard Milk Cartons 61
General Instructions for Working with Milk Cartons 62
   Doorknob Hanger 63
   Prayer Reminder 65
   Bible Story Viewer 66
   Boat 67
   Talking Puppet 69
   Bible-Time House 72
   Harp 73
   Bible Bookmark 74
   Magi Gift Container 75
   Star Luminary 77
   Lacy Candle 78
   Easter Planter 79

Craft Ideas Using Egg Cartons 81
   Advent Calendar 82
   Creatures That Move on the Ground 85
   Lilies of the Field 87
   The Gospel in One Word Is Love 89
   Cross 91
   Jesus' Ascension 92

Reproducible Letter 93

Index 94

Shining Star Publications, Copyright © 1994

SS3805

TO THE TEACHER/PARENT

Each project in this book makes use of recycled materials. The ideas are grouped according to the main material used.

The juice can projects may be created using 12-ounce cans (which hold frozen juice concentrate) or the cans' lids. These lids are removed by pulling a plastic tab, leaving a smooth, rounded edge.

Paper tubes are the cardboard cores in rolls of toilet paper, paper towels, or gift wrap. Tubes vary in length but cut easily with scissors.

The grocery bag projects make use of full-sized brown paper bags which measure approximately 11 1/2" x 16".

Polystyrene trays, commonly called Styrofoam™, are used to package meat, poultry, sliced cheese, and sometimes fruit and vegetables. These trays come in a variety of sizes. If the size is critical to the project, it is listed in the materials section.

All the cardboard milk carton projects are designed to use half-gallon containers. Fruit juice cartons of this size may be used in addition to milk cartons.

Eggs are packaged in polystyrene or cardboard. Unless otherwise stated in the materials list, either material may be used to make the craft.

Any food container needs to be washed and dried before using it in a craft project. Special care must be taken to thoroughly wash in hot, sudsy water trays that have contained meat. A reproducible letter with washing instructions is included at the back of the book, asking families to save these items.

Fifty-nine different craft projects are included in this book. Each may be used to reinforce a Bible story, a biblical theme, or to help celebrate a Christian holiday. Many projects may be used with more than one Bible story. For those ideas, additional story suggestions are listed at the bottom of the page. An index is included to help you locate a craft project to use with a particular Bible story.

The symbol * appears whenever a task needs to be done by an adult. Using a hammer and nail to punch holes, spray painting, and using a hot glue gun are tasks small children should not attempt. Children making these craft items on their own should stop when they see this symbol and ask an adult for help.

GENERAL INSTRUCTIONS FOR DECORATING RECYCLED ITEMS

Juice cans, paper tubes, and cardboard milk cartons may be spray painted with enamel paint. Plan to give the item three to four light coats to avoid runs and to thoroughly cover it. A teacher or parent should paint the materials in advance.

Materials may also be covered with:

- Aluminum foil
- Burlap
- Construction paper shapes
- Craft sticks
- Grocery bags, torn into small pieces
- Fabric scraps
- Felt
- Magazine pictures
- Newspaper
- Paper cut to fit*
- Paper towels
- Popsicle™ sticks
- Ribbon
- Rope
- Tissue paper
- Toothpicks
- Twine
- Wallpaper
- Wrapping paper
- Vinyl
- Yarn

* Paper cut to fit may be painted or printed in these ways:

- Chalk drawings
- Crayon rubbings
- Easel painting
- Finger painting
- Fingerprints
- Marble painting
- Prints made with gadgets
- Spatter painting
- Sponge painting
- Straw painting
- String painting
- Watercolor painting

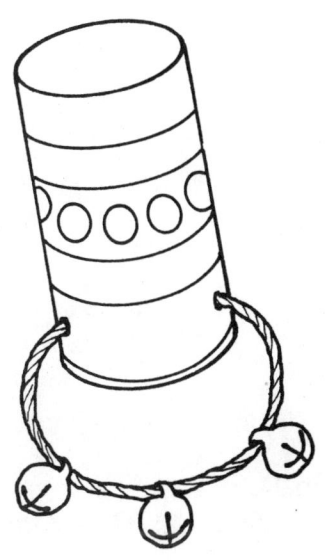  

CRAFT IDEAS USING JUICE CANS AND LIDS

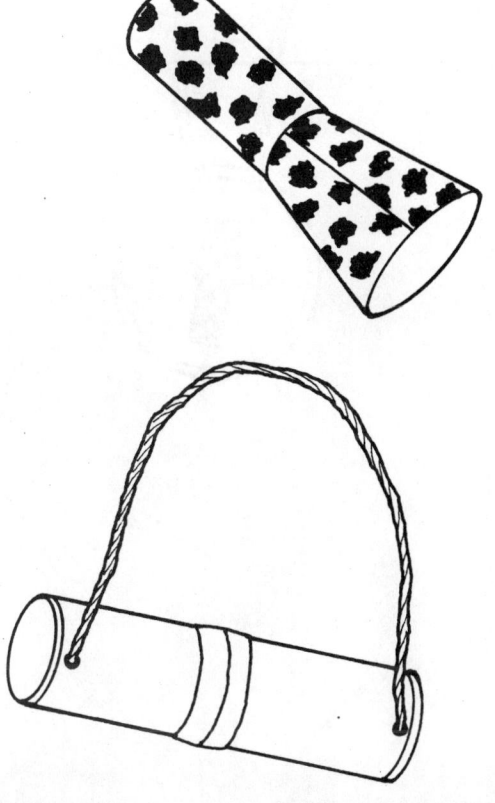  

NATURE PENDANT

"For everything God created is good." 1 Timothy 4:4a

MATERIALS:
Hammer and large nail
Juice can lid
Yarn, twine, or plastic cord
Masking tape
Seeds, pods, nutshells
Glue
Permanent marker

INSTRUCTIONS:
1. * Punch two holes, about 1/2" apart near one edge of the lid (illustration 1).
2. Insert 20" of cord through the holes and tie together the two ends (illustration 2). Cover the rough edges on the back of the lid with masking tape.
3. Gather a variety of natural items to be glued on the pendant. Choose small items that differ in color, texture, and shape. Older children may wish to create a pattern or design (illustration 3).

1

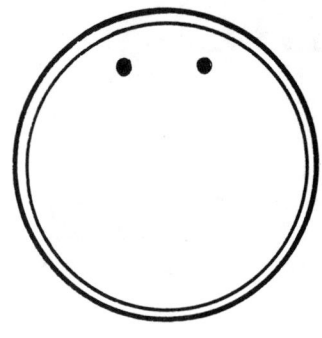

2

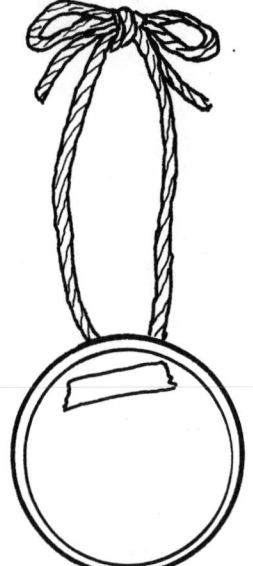

3

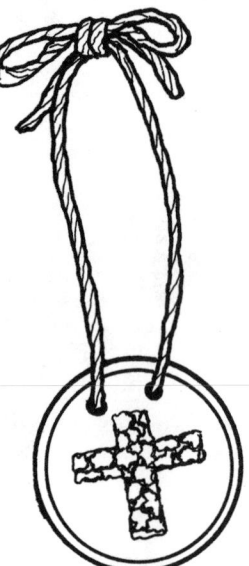

* To be completed by an adult.

ADDITIONAL BIBLE REFERENCES:
Creation (Genesis 1:9-13)
Parable of the Sower (Luke 8:4-15)

MUSICAL INSTRUMENTS
JINGLE CAN

"Praise him with tambourine and dancing, praise him with the strings and flute."   Psalm 150:4

MATERIALS:
Hammer and nail
Juice can
12" pipe cleaner
2-3 bells per child
Masking tape

INSTRUCTIONS:
1. * Punch two holes on opposite sides of the can 1/2" from the base (illustration 1).
2. Decorate can as desired. (See suggestions page 6.)
3. String bells on pipe cleaner (illustration 2). Put each end of the pipe cleaner into opposite holes of the juice can (illustration 3). Bend each end of the pipe cleaner up 2" and tape them inside the can.

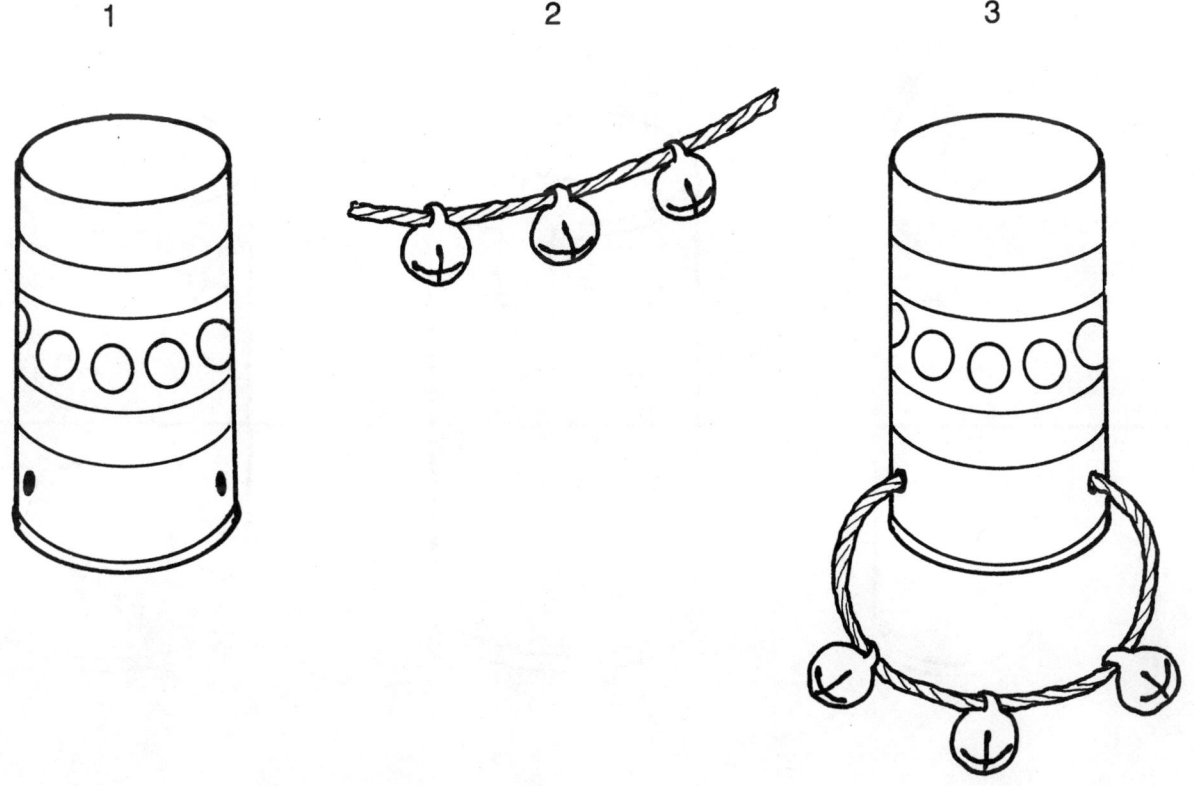

* To be completed by an adult.

MUSICAL INSTRUMENTS
SHAKER

"Make a joyful noise unto the Lord, all ye lands." Psalm 100:1 (KJV)

MATERIALS:
Juice can and lid
Kernels of unpopped corn, dried beans, or macaroni
Masking tape

INSTRUCTIONS:
1. Put a handful of corn, beans, or macaroni in the juice can (illustration 1).
2. Tape lid on can (illustration 2).
3. Decorate can as desired (illustration 3).

1

2

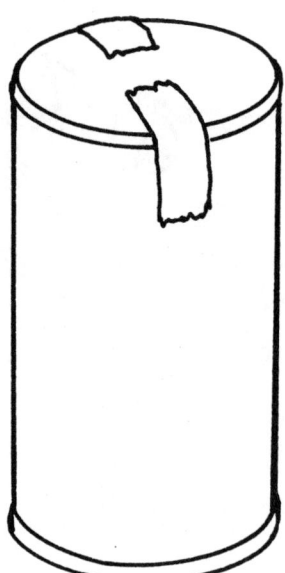

3

MUSICAL INSTRUMENTS CLAPPER

"Praise him with the clash of cymbals, praise him with resounding cymbals."   Psalm 150:5

MATERIALS:
Hammer and large nail
2 juice can lids
3/4" metal washer (available at any hardware store)
7" of 24-gauge craft wire
Masking tape
Permanent markers

INSTRUCTIONS:
1. Decorate the lids with permanent markers (illustration 1).
2. * Hammer the nail through both lids to make a hole. Remove the nail (illustration 2).
3. Thread wire through the hole in one lid, then through the washer, and finally through the last lid. Position the lids so that they are at the midpoint of the wire (illustration 3).
4. Twist the two ends of wire together to form a handle. Wrap the handle with masking tape for safety.

1   2   3

  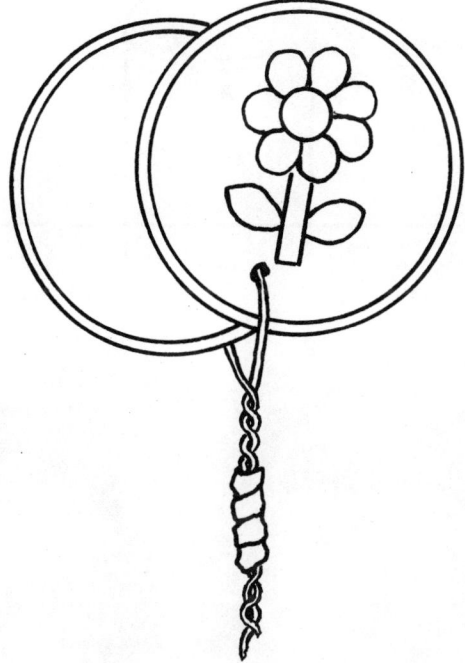

* To be completed by an adult.

MUSICAL INSTRUMENTS
DRUM

"Wake up, wake up, break out in song!" Judges 5:12b

MATERIALS:
Hammer and large nail
2 juice cans
Duct tape
Popsicle™ or craft stick
30" of yarn

INSTRUCTIONS:
1.* Punch one hole near the rim of each juice can (illustration 1).
2. Thread one end of the yarn through the hole and tie a knot on the inside of the can (illustration 2). Tie the other end of the yarn the same way through the second can.
3. Tape the two juice cans together with duct tape (illustration 3).
4. Decorate cans and stick.
5. Drum may be worn over one shoulder and played with fingers or tapped with a craft stick.

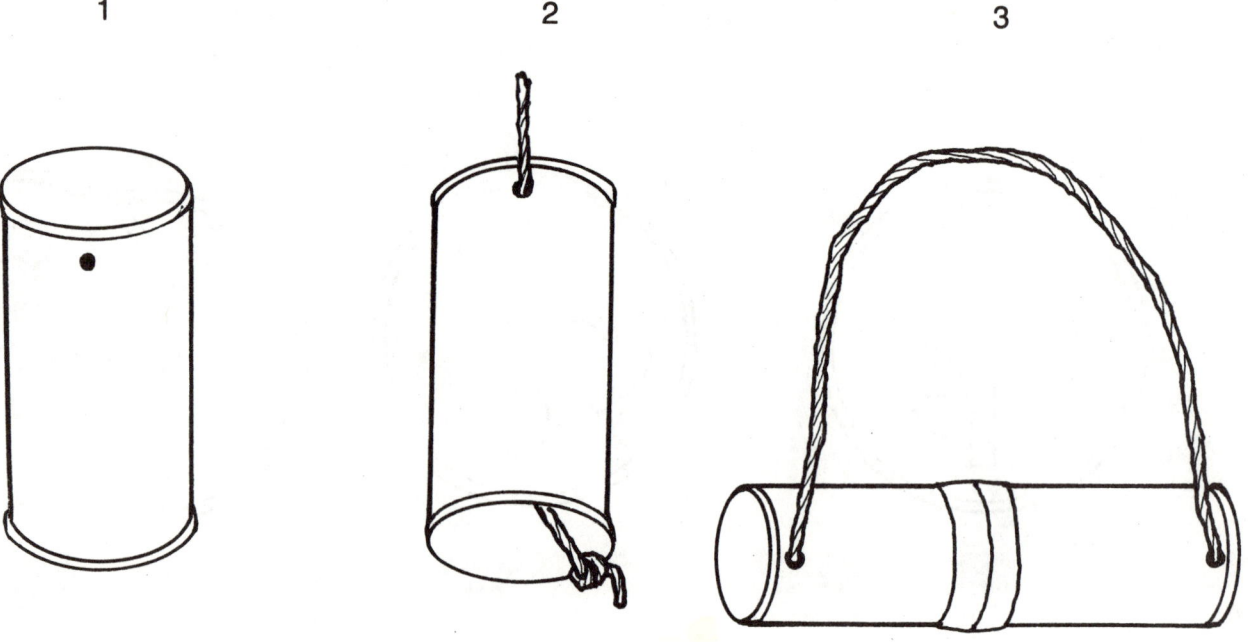

* To be completed by an adult.

MUSICAL INSTRUMENTS
RAM'S HORN

"Have seven priests carry trumpets of rams' horns in front of the ark. On the seventh day, march around the city seven times, with the priests blowing the trumpets."   Joshua 6:4

MATERIALS:
Large screwdriver and hammer
Juice can
Heavy paper
Glue
Beige spray paint
Newspapers
Sponge pieces
Black paint

INSTRUCTIONS:
1. * Use the screwdriver to punch a hole in the metal end of the juice can (illustration 1).
2. Roll paper to form a cone (illustration 2).
3. Dribble glue inside juice can. Put paper cone inside can. Allow to dry.
4. * Cover work area with newspapers, and spray paint can and paper cone beige. Allow to dry.
5. Sponge paint the dry can and cone with black paint to resemble the muted colors of a ram's horn (illustration 3).

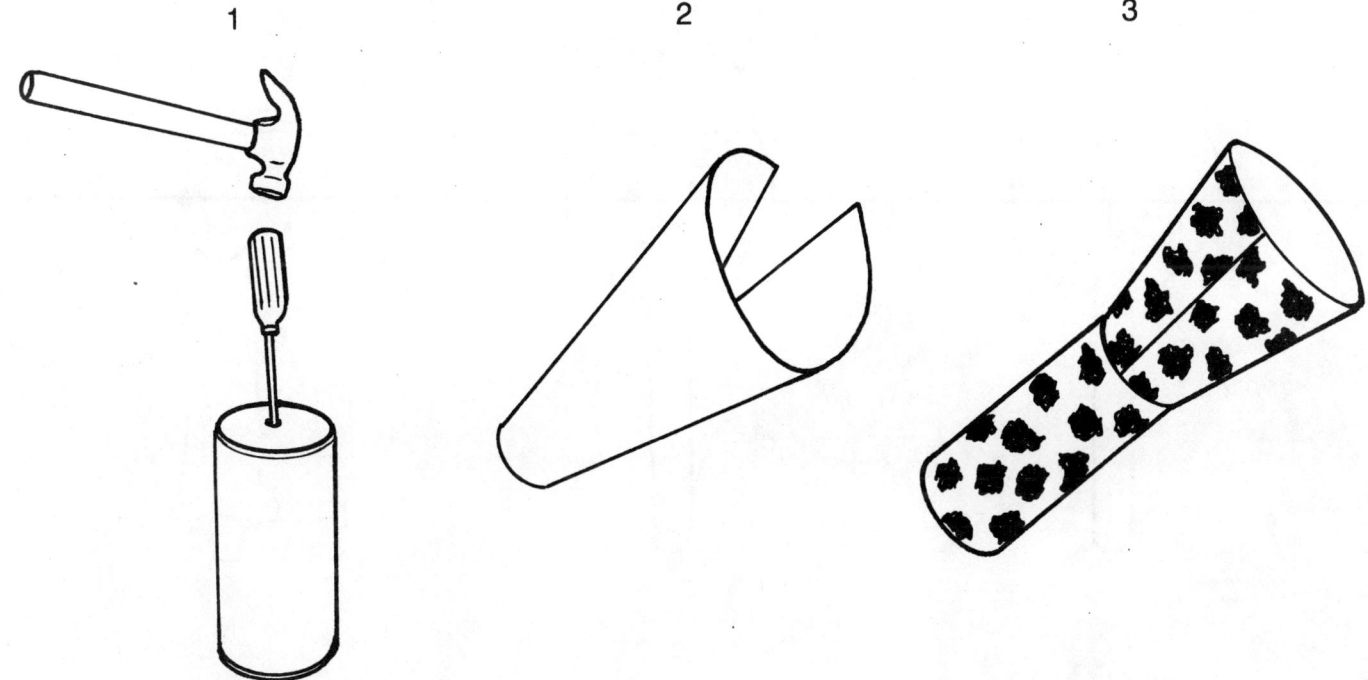

* To be completed by an adult.

ADDITIONAL BIBLE REFERENCES:
Moses at Mt. Sinai (Exodus 19)
Praising God (Psalm 81:1-3)

STICK PUPPETS

"Then Nebuchadnezzar said, 'Praise be to the God of Shadrach, Meshach and Abednego, who has sent his angel and rescued his servants!'"
Daniel 3:28a

MATERIALS:
4 juice can lids
4 craft sticks
Craft glue
Headdress patterns, page 15
Construction paper
Pencil or fine-tip markers
Scissors
Yarn, lace, and fabric scraps

INSTRUCTIONS:
1. Glue the flat side of the lid to one end of a craft stick (illustration 1).
2. While lid is drying, use a second lid to trace and cut four circles from the construction paper.
3. Draw facial features on the circles. Glue one inside each lid.
4. Glue the three remaining lids to the ends of the craft sticks.
5. Use the patterns on page 15 to cut appropriate headwear for each character. Glue in place (illustration 2).
6. Add fabric scraps as clothing for each puppet (illustration 3).

ADDITIONAL BIBLE REFERENCES:
Abraham's Visitors (Genesis 18)
Herod and the Magi (Matthew 2:1-12)
Solomon's Wise Ruling (1 Kings 3:16-28)
Moses and Aaron Go to Pharaoh (Exodus 5:1-12)

STICK PUPPET PATTERNS

ADDITIONAL BIBLE REFERENCES:
Jacob's Ladder (Genesis 28:10-15)
Balaam and His Donkey (Numbers 22:21-35)
Gideon (Judges 6:1-16)
Angel Appears to Zechariah (Luke 1:5-25)
Gabriel Visits Mary (Luke 1:26-38)
Angel at the Tomb (Matthew 28:1-7)
Peter's Rescue (Acts 12:3-10)

Crown for King Nebuchadnezzar

Headdress for Shadrach

Headdress for Meshach

Headdress for Abednego

CHARIOT

"Then Philip ran up to the chariot and heard the man reading Isaiah the prophet."   Acts 8:30a

MATERIALS:
Sturdy scissors
Hammer and Phillips™ screwdriver
Block of wood
Juice can
Grocery bag
2 juice can lids
2 brad fasteners
Tongue depressor
Glue

INSTRUCTIONS:
1. * Cut a U-shaped opening from the juice can (illustration 1).
2. Cut a 4 $3/4$" x 8 $1/2$" rectangle from a brown grocery bag. Glue the rectangle to cover the juice can. Cut the opening from the bag to match the opening in the can.
3. * Punch a hole in the center of each juice can lid with the screwdriver and hammer. Place the lid on the block of wood to protect the table.
4. * Punch a hole on both sides of the juice can near the top and center of the can (illustration 2).
5. Attach the lids to the juice can with brad fasteners. Glue the tongue depressor to the bottom of the juice can for the hitch (illustration 3).

1   2   3

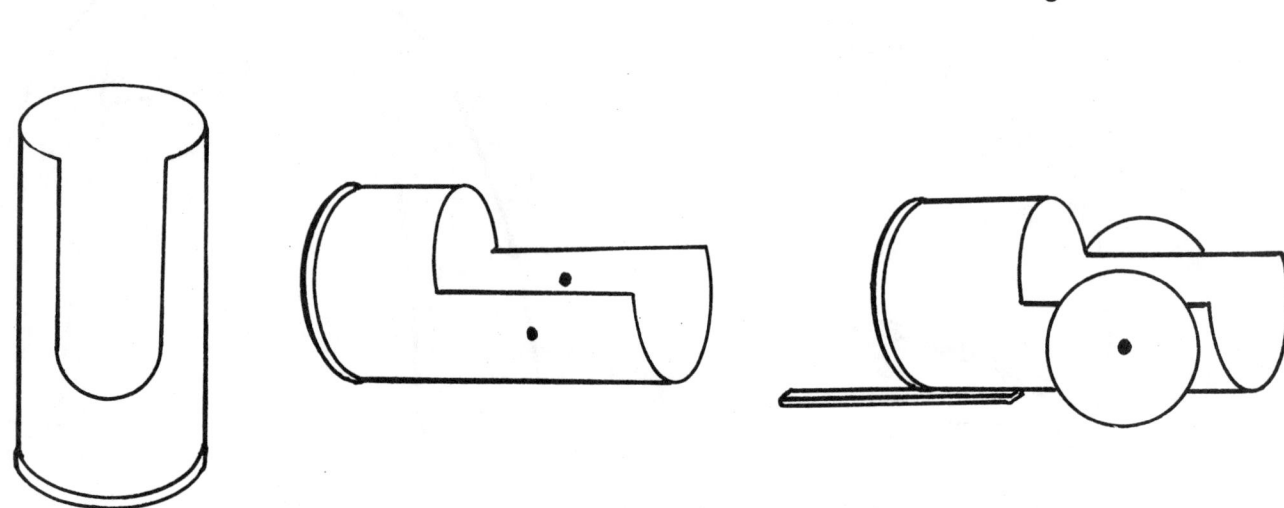

* To be completed by an adult.

ADDITIONAL BIBLE REFERENCES:
Egyptians Pursue the Israelites (Exodus 14)
Solomon's Riches (1 Kings 10:23-29)
Elijah Goes to Heaven (2 Kings 2:11-12)

CHRISTMAS ORNAMENT

Ornaments are used to decorate Christmas trees. The evergreen tree, which never changes color, represents the never-changing love of God.

MATERIALS:
Hammer and large nail
Juice can lids
Masking tape
9" of gathered eyelet or lace per ornament
Glue
Individual picture of each child
Scissors
1/4" x 10" ribbon
Felt
Permanent fine-tip marker

INSTRUCTIONS:
1. Use the lid to trace a circle on your picture, and cut to fit.
2. * Punch a hole near the edge of the lid with the hammer and nail.
3. Cut a piece of ribbon 3" long. Put both ends of the ribbon through the hole. Tape the two ends to the flat back side creating a loop for hanging (illustration 1).
4. Cover the back of the ornament with a piece of felt cut to fit. Add your name and the year with a permanent marker.
5. Glue eyelet or lace to the back of the lid around the edge.
6. Glue your picture to the center (illustration 2).
7. Make a shoestring bow from remaining piece of ribbon and glue it near the hanger (illustration 3).

* To be completed by an adult.

ANGEL

"An angel of the Lord appeared to them, and the glory of the Lord shone around them."

Luke 2:9a

MATERIALS:
Hot glue gun and glue stick
Juice can
Lid
White spray paint
Sturdy scissors
Craft stick, cut in half
Clip-type clothespin
Permanent markers or face pattern
Glue
Glitter and trim (optional)

Face Pattern

INSTRUCTIONS:
1. * Cut a 2 1/2" slit in the can. From the bottom of the slit make a cut at a 45-degree angle back to within 1" of the top edge of the can (illustration 1). Make a second cut on the other side of the slit in the same manner. Bend both cut pieces back to form wings (illustration 2).
2. Flatten the back of the can slightly. * Glue the lid to the front of the stick for the angel's head. Glue the craft stick to the center back of the can. Use a clip-type clothespin to hold lid to can until it dries.
3. * Spray paint the angel. Let dry.
4. Add a face to the angel, using permanent markers or by reproducing the face pattern and gluing it to the lid (illustration 3).
5. Glue on glitter and trim if desired.

1   2   3

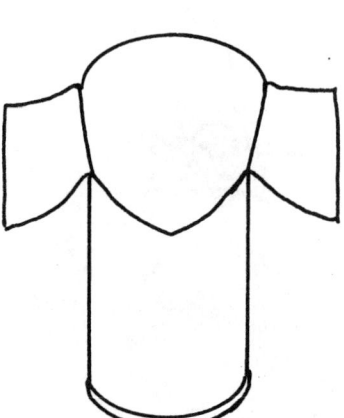

* To be completed by an adult.

NATIVITY SET

"So they hurried off and found Mary and Joseph, and the baby, who was lying in the manger."
Luke 2:16

MATERIALS:
Sturdy scissors
3 juice cans
Felt (light and dark blue, light and bright pink, cream, gold, and brown)
Patterns, pages 20-21
Glue
Ribbon, trim (optional)
Fine-tip markers

INSTRUCTIONS:
1. Using the patterns on pages 20-21, cut the pieces out of felt.
2. Glue the front and back body parts together. Make sure the bottom remains open to slip over the can. Allow to dry.
3. * With sturdy scissors, cut one can so that it measures 2" tall. This will be the manger. Glue the two manger pieces on the can. Add cream pieces to form the legs of the manger.
4. * Cut an inch off a second can and discard the piece. This will be Mary.
5. Draw facial features for Mary and Joseph with the markers. Glue face, hair, robe, sleeves, and hands on Mary (illustration 1). Glue face, headdress, robe, sleeves, and hands on Joseph (illustration 2).
6. Fringe the gold felt for the hay. Glue to manger.
7. Glue baby's head to the baby's body. Glue figure on hay (illustration 3).
8. Add ribbon and trim to figures if desired.
9. Additional figures may be created using the same patterns but varying the color and trim of the clothes.

1 2 3

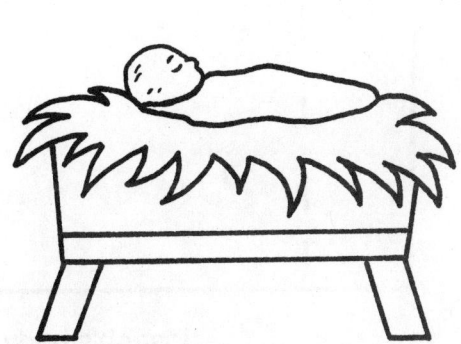

* To be completed by an adult.

ADDITIONAL BIBLE REFERENCE:
Visit of the Magi (Matthew 2:1-11)

NATIVITY PATTERNS

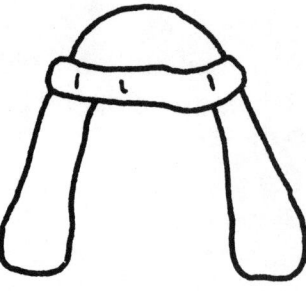

Joseph's headdress
Cut 1

Sleeve from light color
Cut 2 for Mary,
2 for Joseph

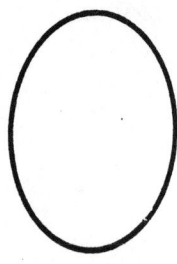

Face
Cut 2

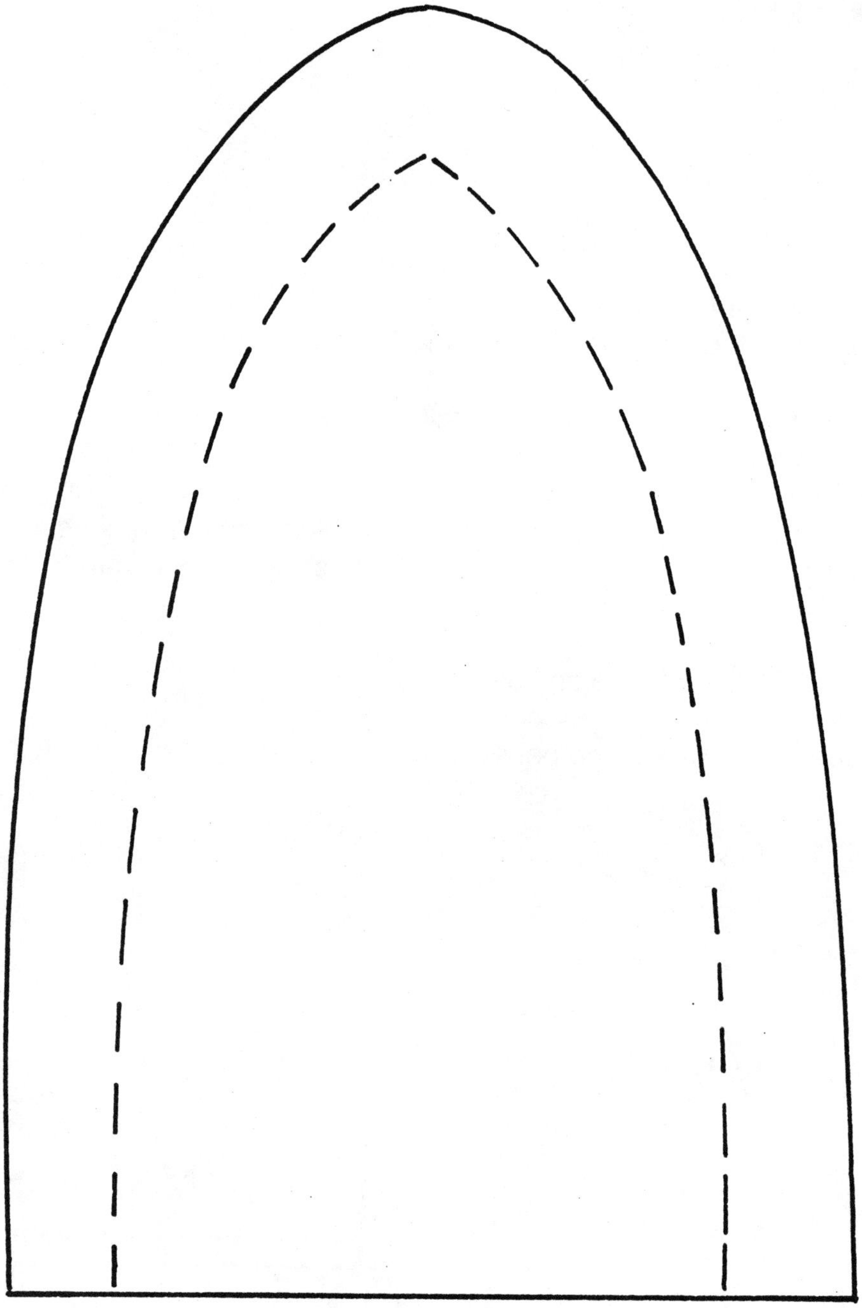

Joseph's body from dark color
Cut 2
(Broken line shows robe cut from light color)
Cut 1

Hand
Cut 4

Shining Star Publications, Copyright © 1994

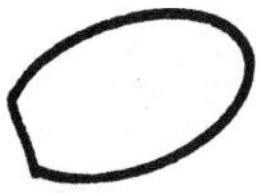

NATIVITY PATTERNS

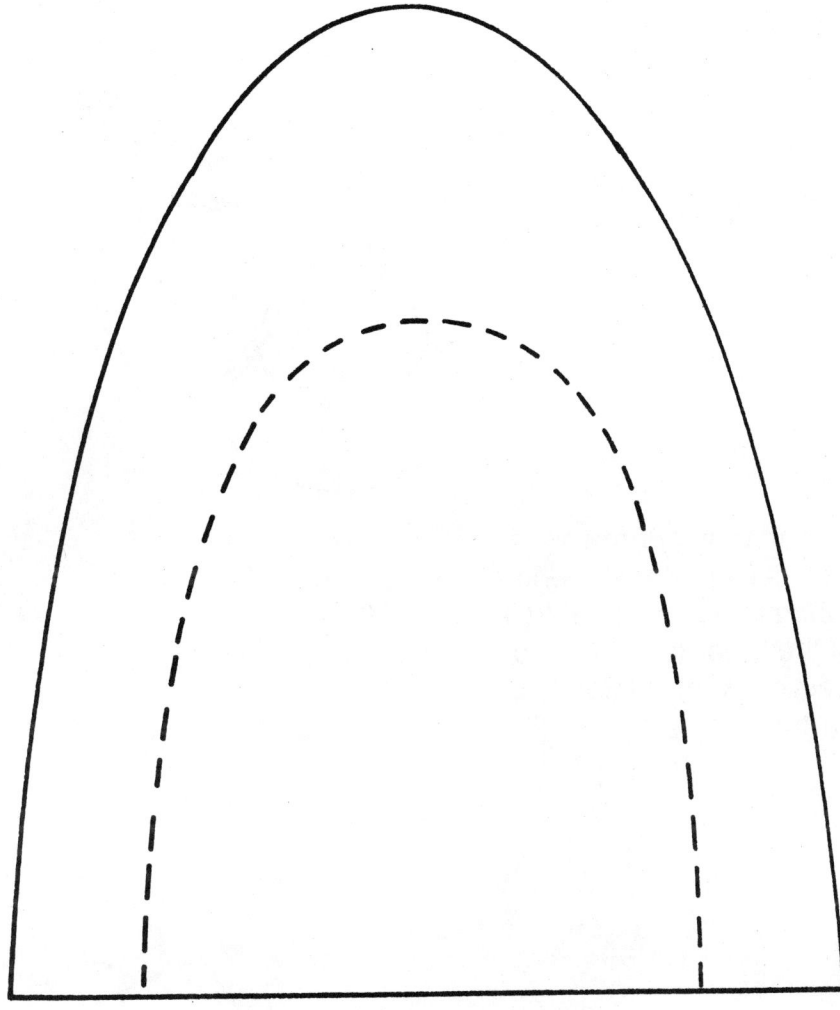

Mary's body from bright color
Cut 2
(Broken line shows robe cut from light color)
Cut 1

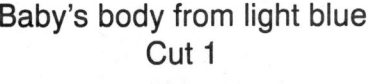
Mary's hair
Cut 1

Baby's body from light blue
Cut 1

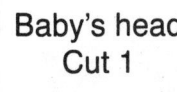
Baby's head
Cut 1

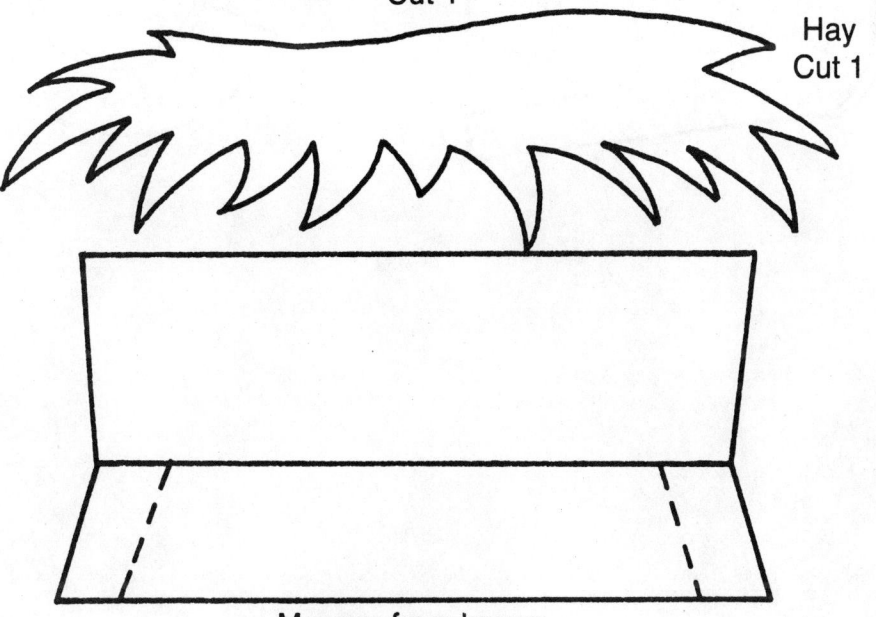

Hay
Cut 1

Manger from brown
Cut 2

EMPTY TOMB

"They found the stone rolled away from the tomb, but when they entered, they did not find the body of the Lord Jesus."

Luke 24:2-3

MATERIALS:
Sturdy scissors
Hammer and large nail
Block of wood
Juice can lid
Juice can
Large brad fastener
Spray paint (gray or brown)

INSTRUCTIONS:
1.* Spray the outside of the juice can gray or brown.
2.* Cut three 1" slits an equal distance apart in the end of the can (illustration 1).
3. Bend back two sections. The third remains straight (illustration 2).
4.* Punch a hole near the rim of the lid large enough for the brad to go through.
5.* Punch a hole in one of the sections that is folded back.
6. Attach the lid to the can with the brad fastener (illustration 3). Lid should be able to roll away.

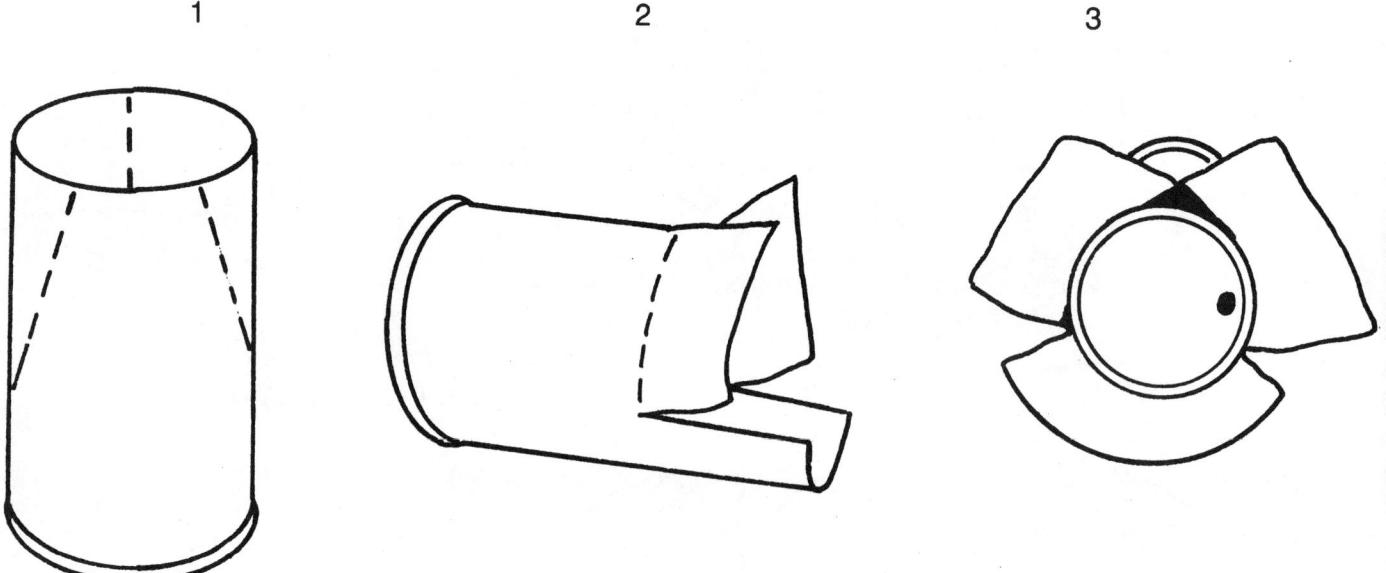

* To be completed by an adult.

MINI EASTER BASKET

Children may use these baskets to explain to others what Easter really is. The cross represents Jesus' death. The stone represents the stone that was rolled away from His empty tomb.

MATERIALS:
Sturdy scissors
Hammer and nail
Juice can
Pipe cleaner
Masking tape
Items to decorate outside of can
Easter grass and symbols (small cross and a
   round stone)

INSTRUCTIONS:
1. * Cut 2" off the juice can to make it shorter.
2. * Punch two holes on opposite sides of the juice can 1/2" from top edge (illustration 1).
3. Decorate can as desired.
4. Force one end of the pipe cleaner through each hole. Bend ends up inside the can and tape to secure the handle in place (illustration 2).
5. Add Easter grass, cross, and stone (illustration 3).

1
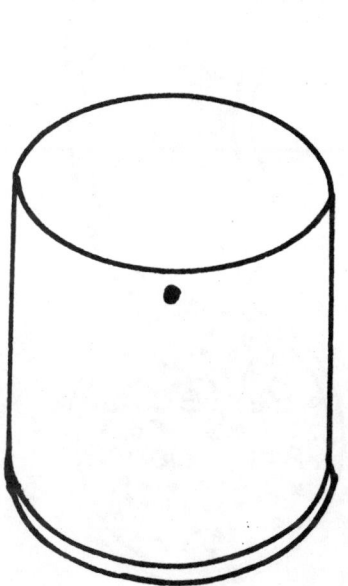

2

3

* To be completed by an adult.

AWARD DAY MEDAL

The Lord has promised to reward those who faithfully serve Him. We sometimes receive awards here on earth, but His will be much greater!

MATERIALS:
2 juice can lids
Glue
30" of ribbon
Paper
Scissors
Fine-tip marker
Glitter

INSTRUCTIONS:
1. Glue the lids together back-to-back with both ends of the ribbon between them (illustration 1).
2. Cut the paper to fit inside one side of the lids.
3. Print the name of the award on the paper (illustration 2).
4. Glue paper inside one lid, and decorate award with glitter (illustration 3).

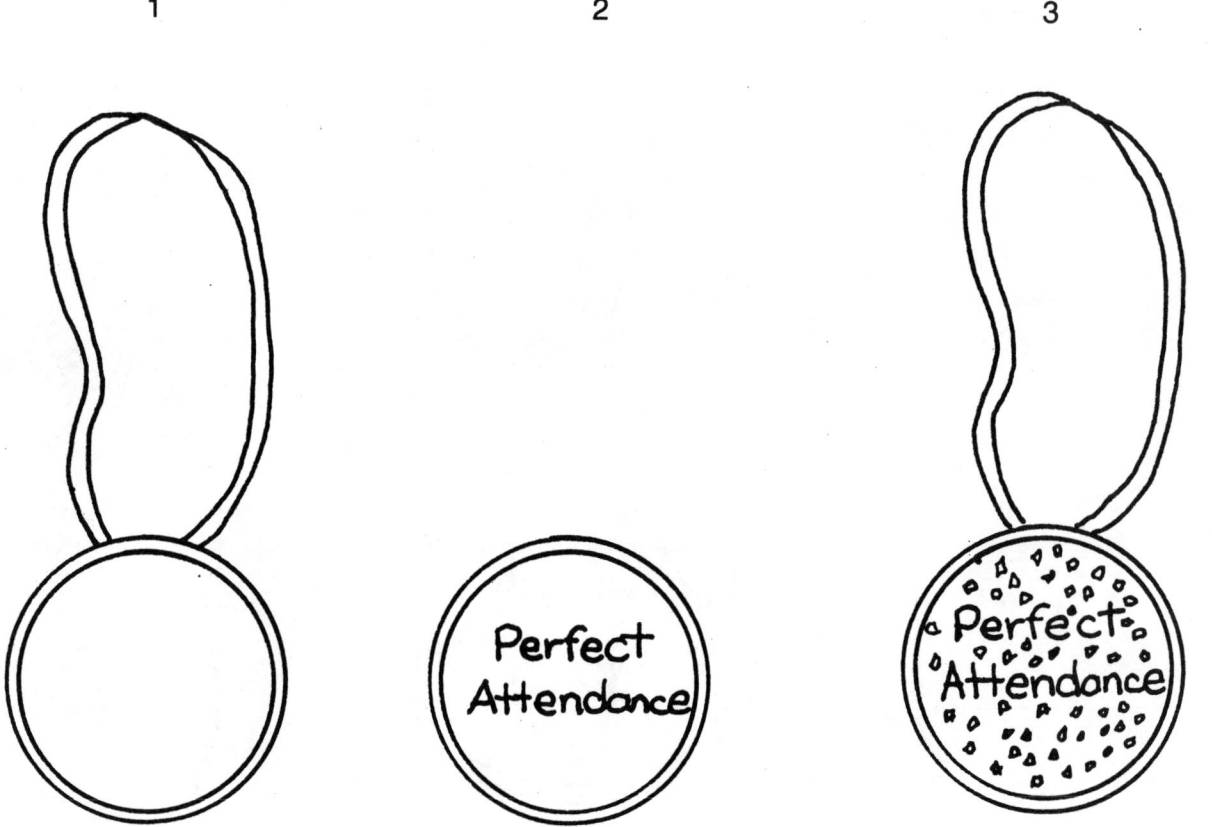

PRAYER MAGNET

"[Give] thanks to God the Father for everything, in the name of our Lord Jesus Christ."
Ephesians 5:20

MATERIALS:
Juice can lid
2" strip of magnetic tape
Glitter
Glue
Praying hands pattern
Felt
Scissors
Bible words
Paper

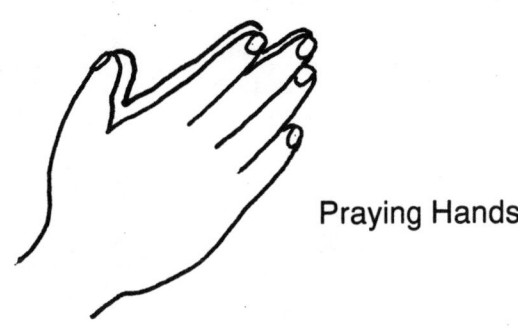

Praying Hands

INSTRUCTIONS:
1. Attach the magnetic strip to the flat side of the lid.
2. Glue glitter to the top of the lid. Completely cover the area inside the rim.
3. While the glitter is drying, use the pattern above to cut praying hands from felt.
4. Make a copy of the Bible message below (illustration 1) or print it on a 1 ½" x ½" strip of paper.
5. Glue the felt hands in the center of the glittered lid (illustration 2).
6. Glue the Bible message on the hands (illustration 3).

1   2   3

Give thanks for everything!

ADDITIONAL BIBLE REFERENCES:
God's Provision (Acts 14:17)
Giving Thanks (1 Thessalonians 5:16-18)

JESUS, THE LIGHT OF THE WORLD

"The light shines in the darkness." John 1:5a

MATERIALS:
Hot glue gun and glue sticks
Hammer and nail
Scrap of wood
Cross pattern
Paper
Scissors
Tape
Juice can lid
Night-light with removable shade

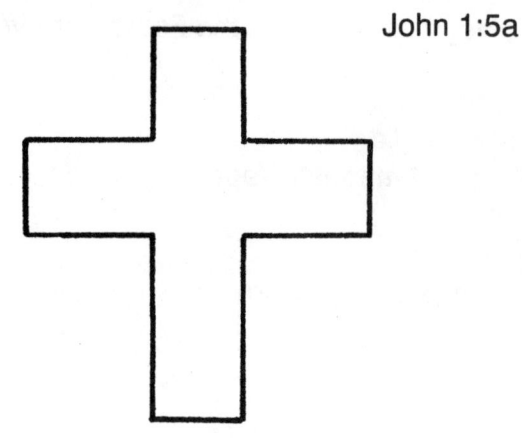

Cross Pattern

INSTRUCTIONS:
1. Reproduce and cut the cross from paper; then tape it inside the lid (illustration 1).
2.* Place the lid on top of the wood scrap. Use the hammer and nail to punch holes outlining the cross (illustration 2). Remove the paper pattern.
3.* Remove the plastic shade from the night-light. Position the hole-punched lid in front of the bulb. Glue the lid to the base of the light. Hold in place until glue sets (illustration 3).

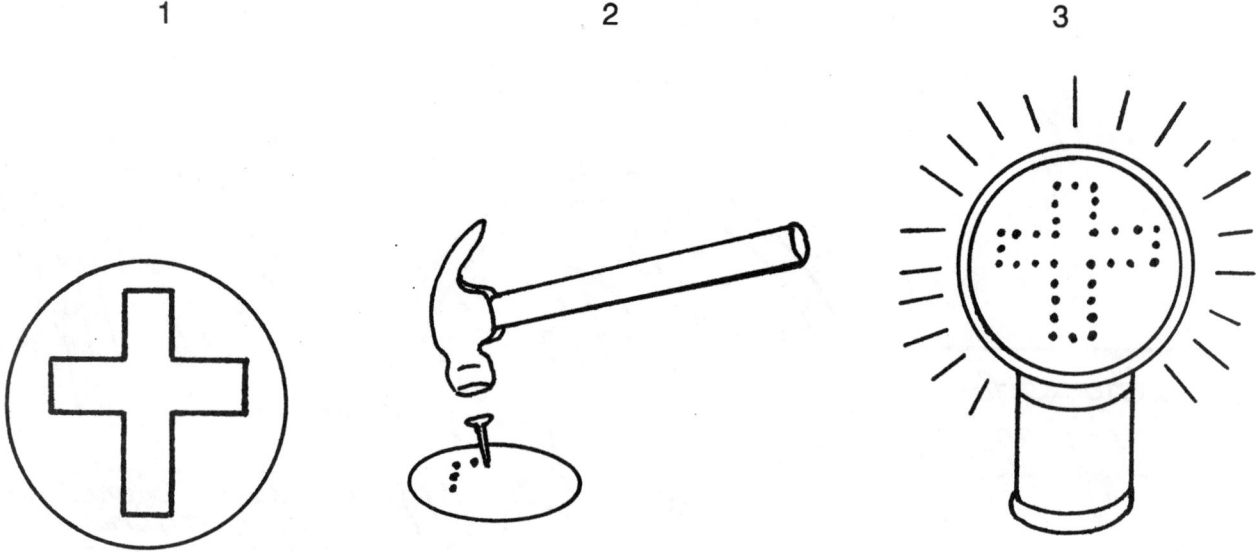

1   2   3

* To be completed by an adult.

ADDITIONAL BIBLE REFERENCES:
God Creates Light (Genesis 1:3-4)
God Is My Light (2 Samuel 22:29)
God Turns Darkness to Light (Psalm 18:28)

 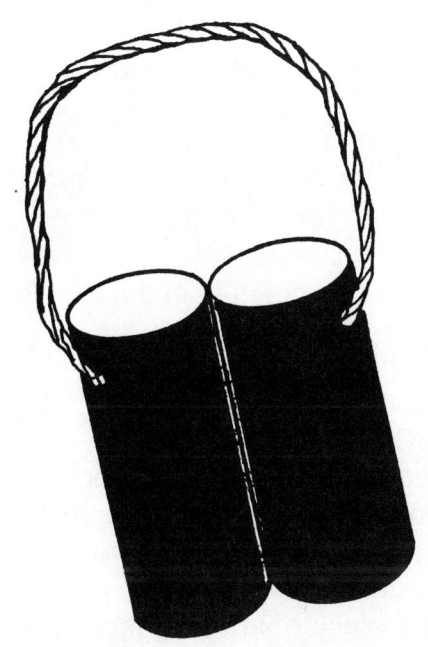

CRAFT IDEAS USING PAPER TUBES

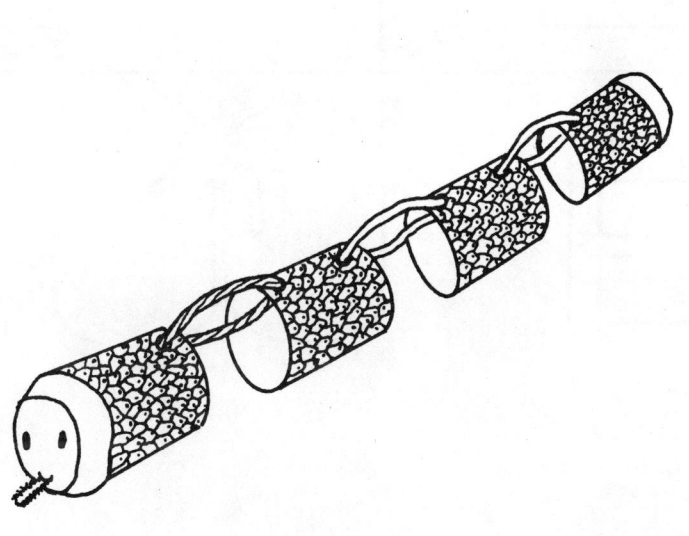 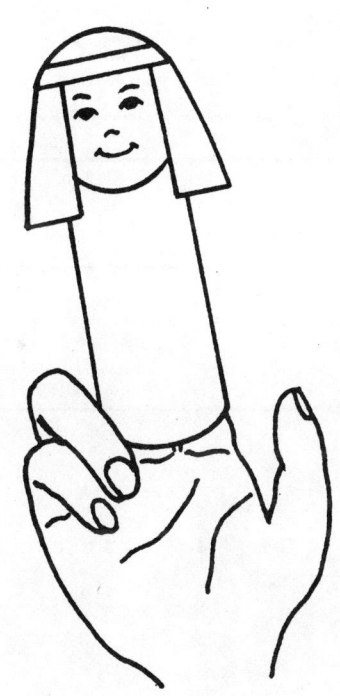

SCROLL–THE BIBLE JESUS KNEW

"The scroll of the prophet Isaiah was handed to him." Luke 4:17a

MATERIALS:
Shelf paper or wide paper used for calculators
2 toilet paper tubes per child
Wide masking tape
Selected Bible verses from the Old Testament
Crayons (optional)
Yarn

INSTRUCTIONS:
1. Cut paper into a piece 18" long and 4 $1/2$" wide.
2. In large letters, print a Bible verse or phrase on the strip of paper (illustration 1). Younger children may draw pictures to represent Bible stories. Since Hebrew reads from right to left, older children may have fun printing the Bible verse in reverse order.
3. Place a piece of masking tape at each end of the length of paper. Lay the paper tube on the masking tape, taping the paper to the tube (illustration 2). Roll each tube toward the middle.
4. Tie with yarn (illustration 3).

ADDITIONAL BIBLE REFERENCES:
The Lost Book Is Found (2 Kings 21:1-23:25; 2 Chronicles 33:1-35:27)
Moses Records the Defeat of the Amalekites (Exodus 17:8-16)
Jehoiakim Burns Jeremiah's Scroll (Jeremiah 36)

ARK ANIMALS

"Two of every kind of bird, of every kind of animal and of every kind of creature that moves along the ground will come to you to be kept alive." Genesis 6:20

MATERIALS:
Paper tubes
Scissors
Tagboard or poster board
Animal patterns, page 30
Markers
Scissors
4 3/4" x 8 1/2" construction paper (various animal colors)
Glue
Wiggle eyes
Yarn
Felt scraps
Pencil

INSTRUCTIONS:
1. Trace each animal pattern on tagboard or poster board, and cut it out.
2. Cut a paper tube to represent the size of the animal. Use a full-length tube for an elephant, but a shorter tube for sheep.
3. Choose an appropriate color of construction paper, and glue it around the paper tube.
4. Hold the tube in the center of the back of the animal body and trace around it to make a circle (illustration 1). Lift the tube off and squeeze a thick line of glue on the circle line (illustration 2). Place the tube in the glue and let it stand.
5. Glue the front body piece to the other end of the tube while it is standing on end (illustration 3). Allow it to dry.
6. Add a yarn tail, felt ears, wiggle eyes, and other features to finish the animal. Make pairs of animals to board the ark.

1
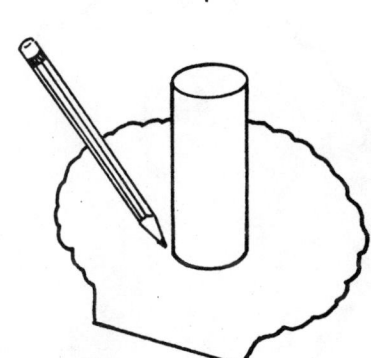

2
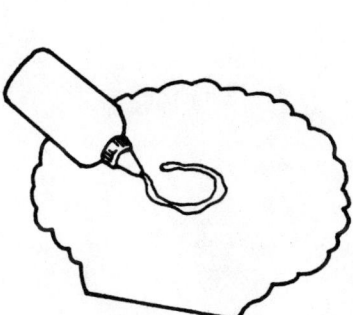

3
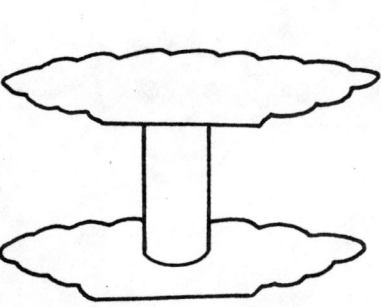

ARK ANIMAL PATTERNS

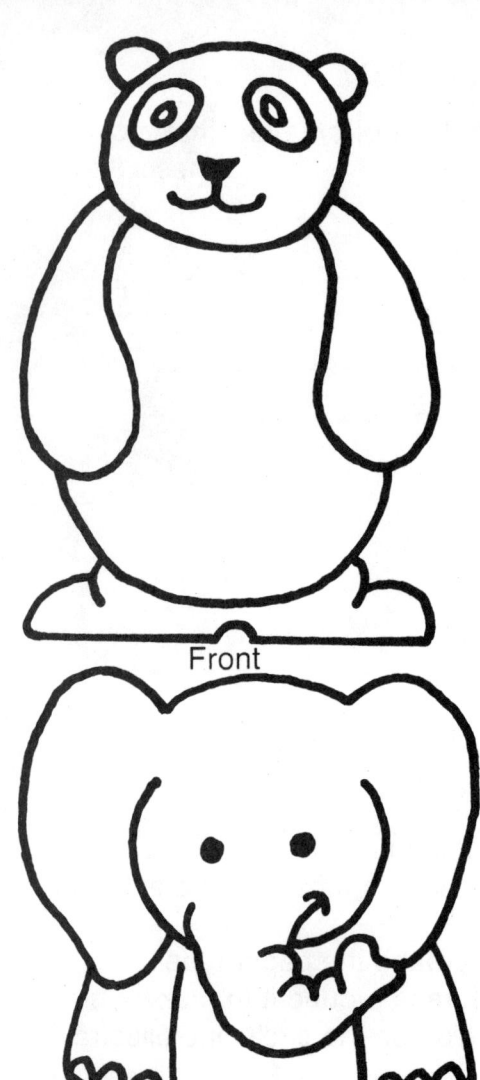

ADDITIONAL BIBLE REFERENCES:
Balaam and His Donkey (Numbers 22:21-35), Jesus' Triumphant Entry (Mark 11:1-11), Jesus, the Good Shepherd (John 10:11-16), Daniel in the Lions' Den (Daniel 6), Samson (Judges 14:5-18)

Shining Star Publications, Copyright © 1994   30   SS3805

SERPENT

"Now the serpent was more crafty than any of the wild animals the Lord God had made."

Genesis 3:1a

MATERIALS:
Sturdy scissors
Paper tubes
Hole punch
Markers
Yarn
Cardboard egg carton sections
Glue
Tiny wiggle eyes
Red pipe cleaner

INSTRUCTIONS:
1. * Cut the paper tubes into sections approximately 1 1/2" in length. Punch a hole near both ends of the middle section (illustration 1). The front and rear sections will each have only one hole punched.
2. Decorate each section with markers to resemble snakeskin (illustration 2).
3. Tie the sections together with short pieces of yarn.
4. Glue a single egg carton section to each end. Add eyes and pipe cleaner mouth to one end (illustration 3).

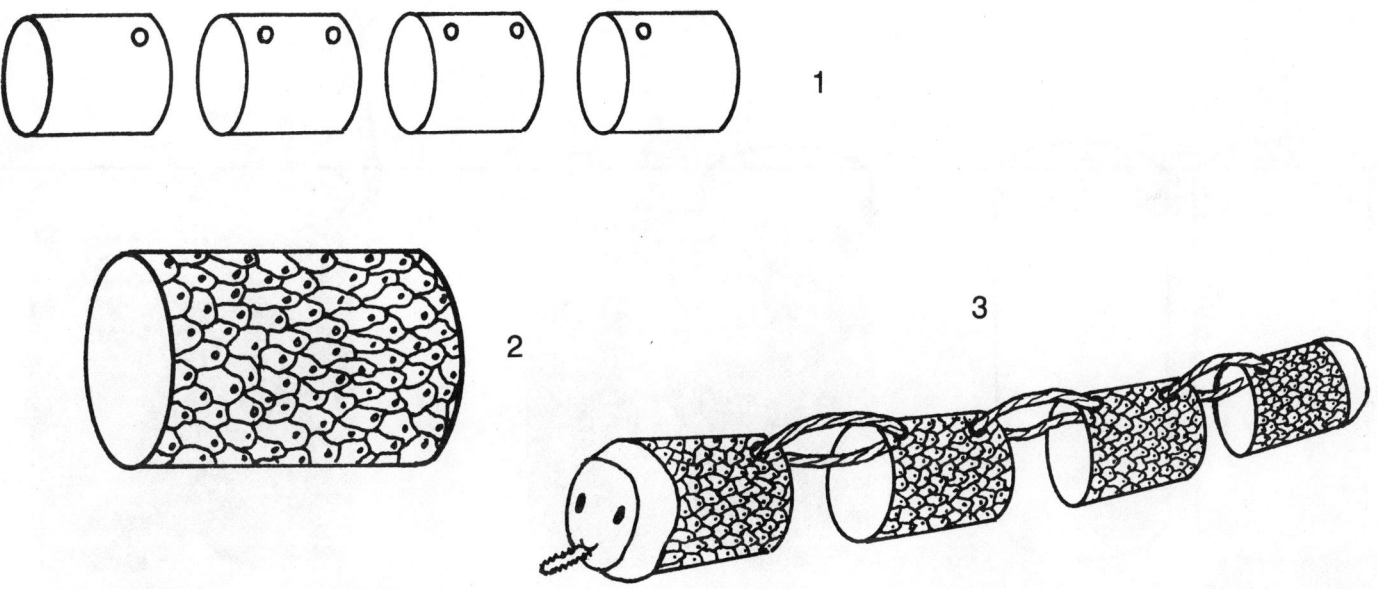

* To be completed by an adult.

ADDITIONAL BIBLE REFERENCES:
Exodus 7:12
Matthew 10:16b

CREATION VIEWER

"Through him all things were made." John 1:3a

MATERIALS:
2 paper tubes
Hole punch
28" piece of yarn
Black paint and brush
Glue
Rubber band

INSTRUCTIONS:
1. Punch one hole in each tube about 1/2" from the end (illustration 1).
2. Paint both tubes black. Allow them to dry.
3. Glue the two tubes together (illustration 2). Hold in place with a rubber band until the glue dries.
4. Tie one end of the yarn through each hole (illustration 3). These "viewers" may be worn around the neck to look at all God created.

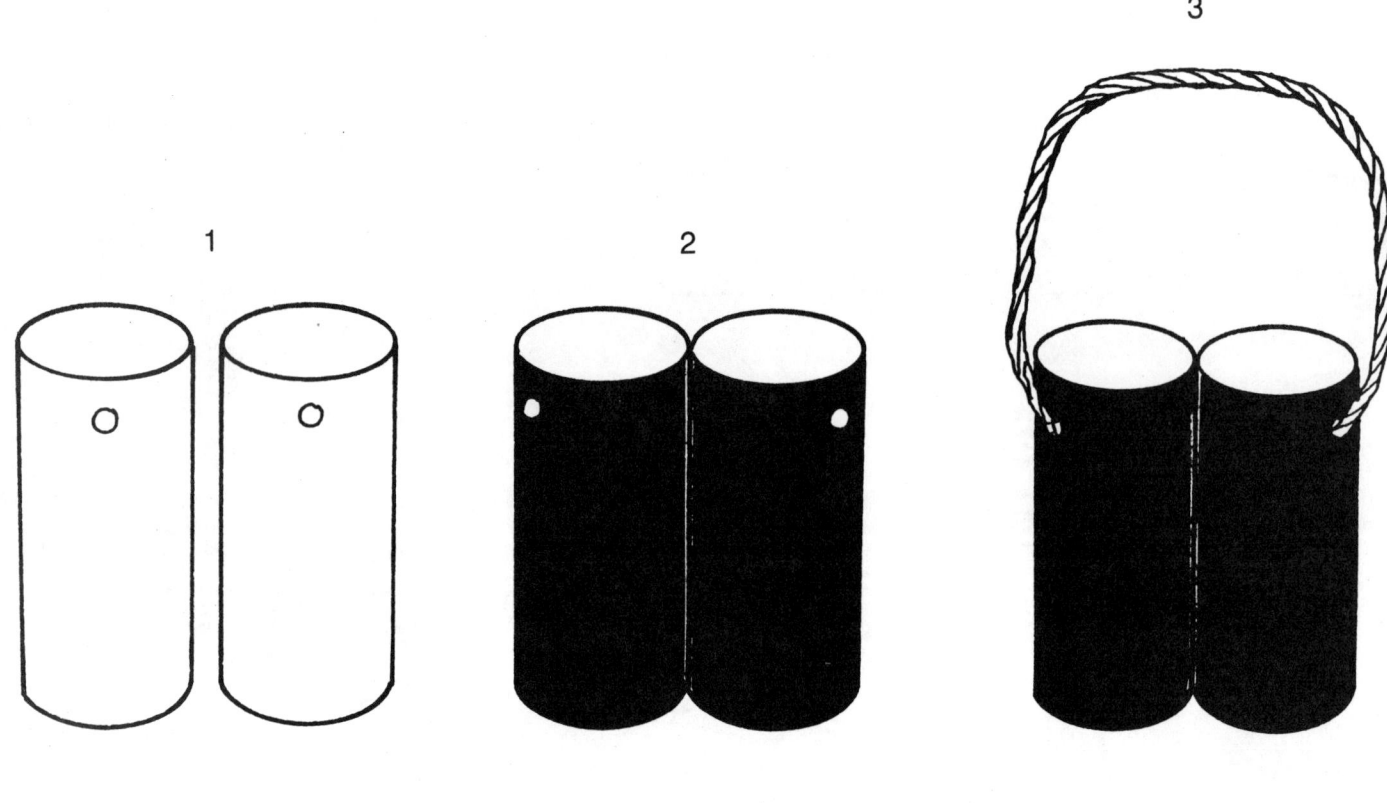

ADDITIONAL BIBLE REFERENCE:
Creation (Genesis 1–2)

CENTURION

"When Jesus had entered Capernaum, a centurion came to him, asking for help."
Matthew 8:5

MATERIALS:
Paper tube
Centurion pattern, page 34
Crayons
Aluminum foil
Flat crepe paper
Egg carton
Pipe cleaner
Scissors
Glue

INSTRUCTIONS:
1. Reproduce the centurion pattern on page 34. Color it, cut it out, and glue it around the tube (illustration 1).
2. Glue on a piece of aluminum foil for his armor.
3. Make a cape from crepe paper by cutting a rectangle approximately 4" x 3". Gather the top of the longer edge and glue it to the back of the soldier (illustration 2).
4. Make the centurion's helmet from a corner egg carton section. The square point will be centered between the centurion's eyes. Add a 3" piece of pipe cleaner to the top. Bend it forward and back to add design to the helmet (illustration 3).

1
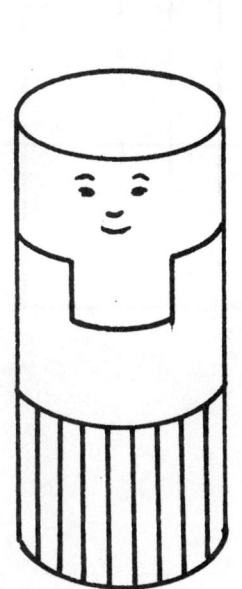

2
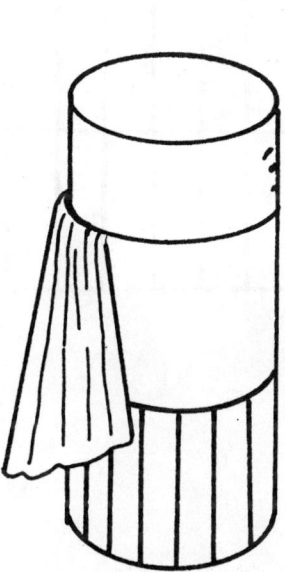

3

ADDITIONAL BIBLE REFERENCES:
Jesus' Death (Matthew 27:45-54)
Peter and Cornelius (Acts 10)
Plot to Kill Paul (Acts 23:12-35)

CENTURION PATTERN

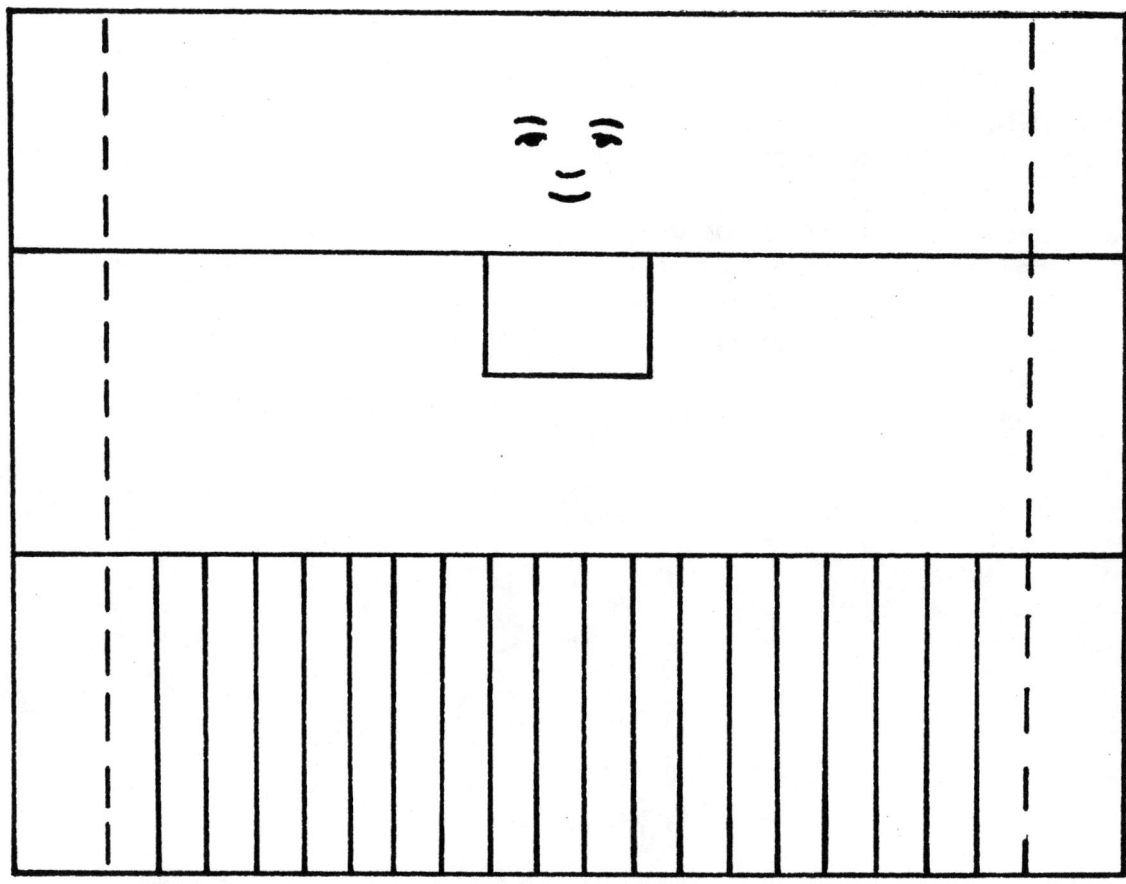

FINGER PUPPET

"But Lot's wife looked back, and she became a pillar of salt."   Genesis 19:26

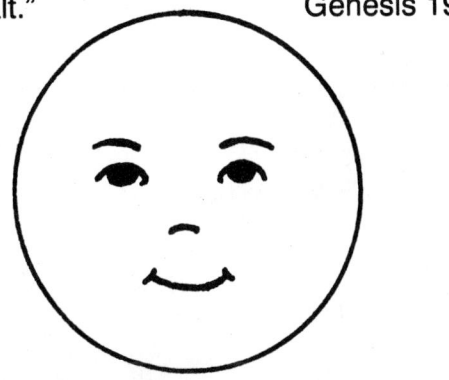

Face Pattern

MATERIALS:
Paper tube
Tempera paint and brush
Face pattern from this page
Paper
Scissors
Glue
Construction paper

INSTRUCTIONS:
1. Paint the paper tube and allow it to dry.
2. Use the face pattern to make a face and headdress for the puppet (illustration 1).
3. Cut out the face, and glue it to one end of the tube. Make a headdress out of construction paper, and glue to the face (illustration 2).
4. Operate the puppet by inserting two fingers inside the tube (illustration 3).
5. Construction paper arms may be glued to the sides of the tube if desired.

1   2   3

  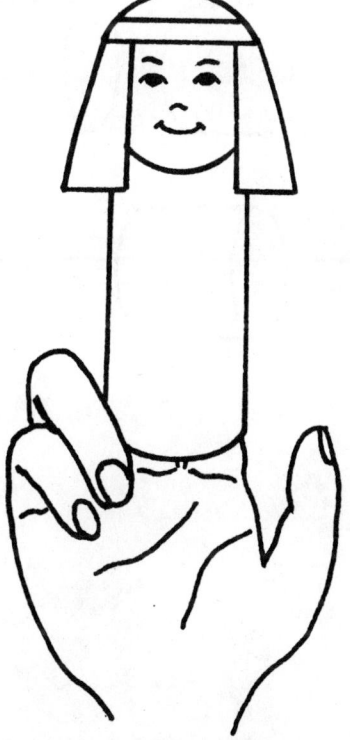

ADDITIONAL BIBLE REFERENCES:
Tower of Babel (Genesis 11:1-9)
Joseph Sold as a Slave (Genesis 37:12-36)
Crossing the Red Sea (Exodus 13:17-14:31)

THANKSGIVING NAPKIN RINGS

"Now, our God, we give you thanks, and praise your glorious name." 1 Chronicles 29:13

MATERIALS:
Sturdy scissors
Paper tubes
Kernels of dry corn or unpopped popcorn
Glue
Egg cartons
Gold spray paint

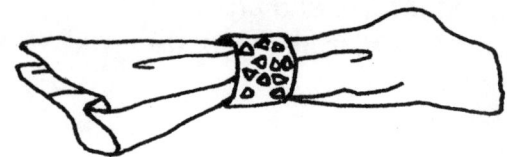

INSTRUCTIONS:
1. * Cut the paper tubes into 1" sections (illustration 1). Design a section for each dinner guest expected for Thanksgiving.
2. Put each length of tube in one egg carton section (illustration 2). This prevents the tube from rolling while it is being decorated.
3. Glue kernels of corn to the rings (illustration 3). The seeds remind us of the first winter the Pilgrims spent in America when food was so scarce they had just a small amount to eat. They also remind us how God causes food to grow from tiny seeds.
4. * Spray paint each napkin ring.

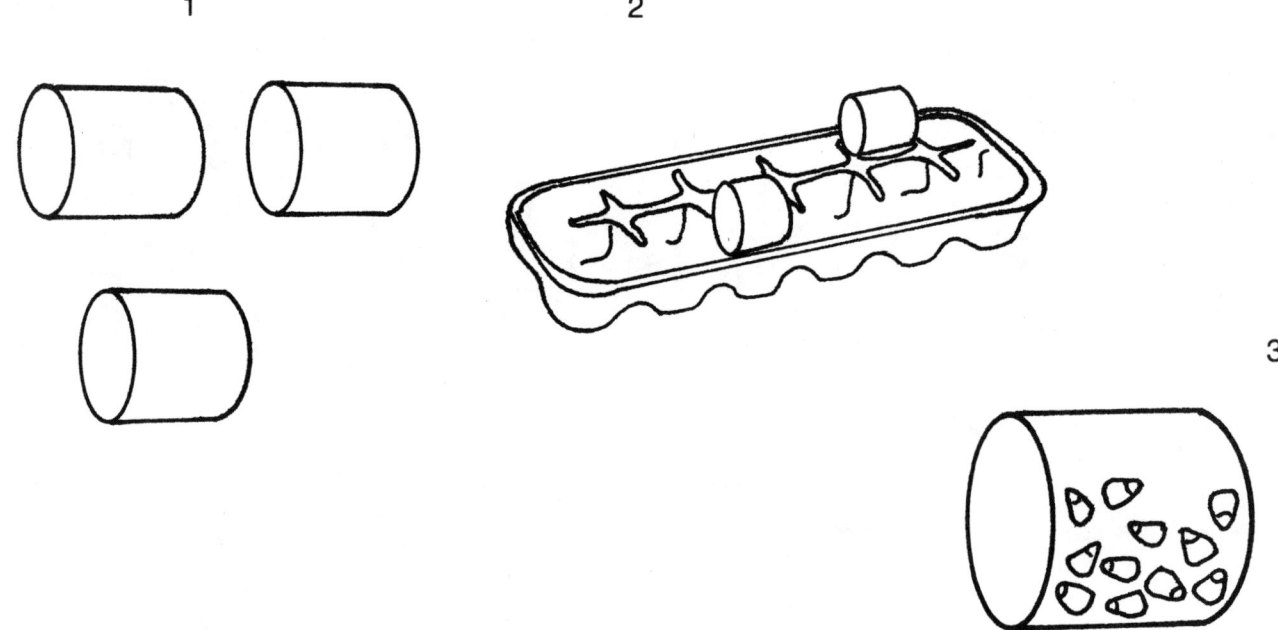

* To be completed by an adult.

ADDITIONAL BIBLE REFERENCES:
Thanking God (Psalm 95:2a)
Give Thanks to God (1 Chronicles 16:34)
Receiving God's Gifts with Thanksgiving (1 Timothy 4:4)

ADVENT CANDLES

The candles represent Jesus who is the light in our dark world. One candle is lit the first Sunday, two on the second Sunday, and so forth. The light grows brighter each week just as our anticipation of the Christ Child grows.

MATERIALS:
5 paper tubes per child
Scissors
5 cardboard circles 1 3/4" in diameter
Paint and paintbrush
Glue
Glitter
Flame pattern on this page
Yellow tissue paper
Polystyrene tray
Masking tape
Construction paper for holly leaves and berries (optional)

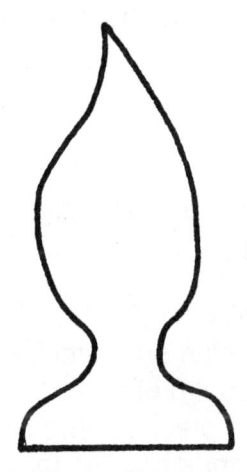

Flame Pattern

INSTRUCTIONS:
1. * Cut four 1/2" slits an equal distance apart in one end of each tube. Fold the tabs out so the tube will stand (illustration 1).
2. Glue a cardboard circle to the other end of each tube (illustration 2).
3. Place one hand inside the open end of the tube to hold it as you paint the tube and the cardboard circle.
4. Sprinkle on glitter when paint is nearly dry.
5. Tape the five candles to a large polystyrene tray (illustration 3). Add construction paper greenery, if desired.
6. Using the pattern on this page, cut five flames from tissue paper.
7. Twist base of flames. Take the candles and five flames home.
8. Your family may tape the flame to the top of one candle each week. You may wish to take home a short family devotion to be read when each candle is "lit." The fifth candle is "lit" on Christmas Day.

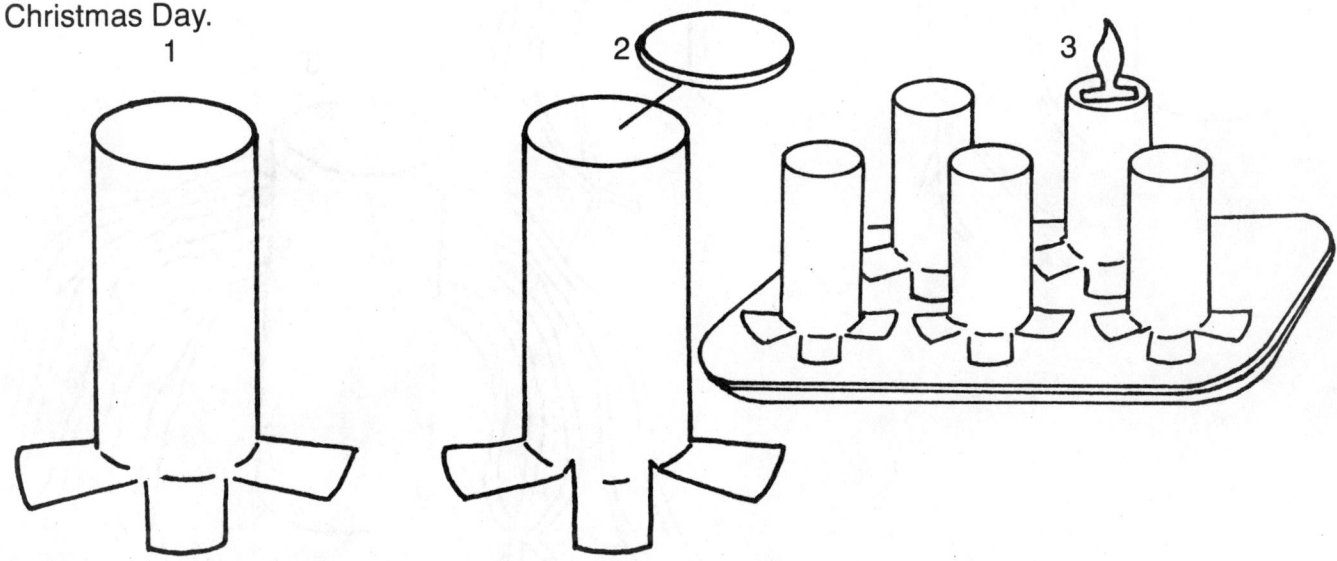

* To be completed by an adult.

PALM BRANCH

"They took palm branches and went out to meet him, shouting, 'Hosanna!'" John 12:13a

MATERIALS:
Green raffia (stringy, straw-like fiber available at craft stores)
Scissors
Paper towel tube
Masking tape
Brown grocery bag (optional)
Glue (optional)

INSTRUCTIONS:
1. * Cut two 3" slits on opposite sides of the paper tube (illustration 1). The tube serves as the stem for the palm branch.
2. Cut raffia into pieces approximately 24" in length.
3. Slide the strands of raffia through both slits in the tube (illustration 2).
4. Place a piece of masking tape over the top edges of the slits to keep raffia from coming out (illustration 3).
5. Tear small pieces of the brown grocery bag and glue them to the paper tube to resemble the rough bark of a tree, if desired.

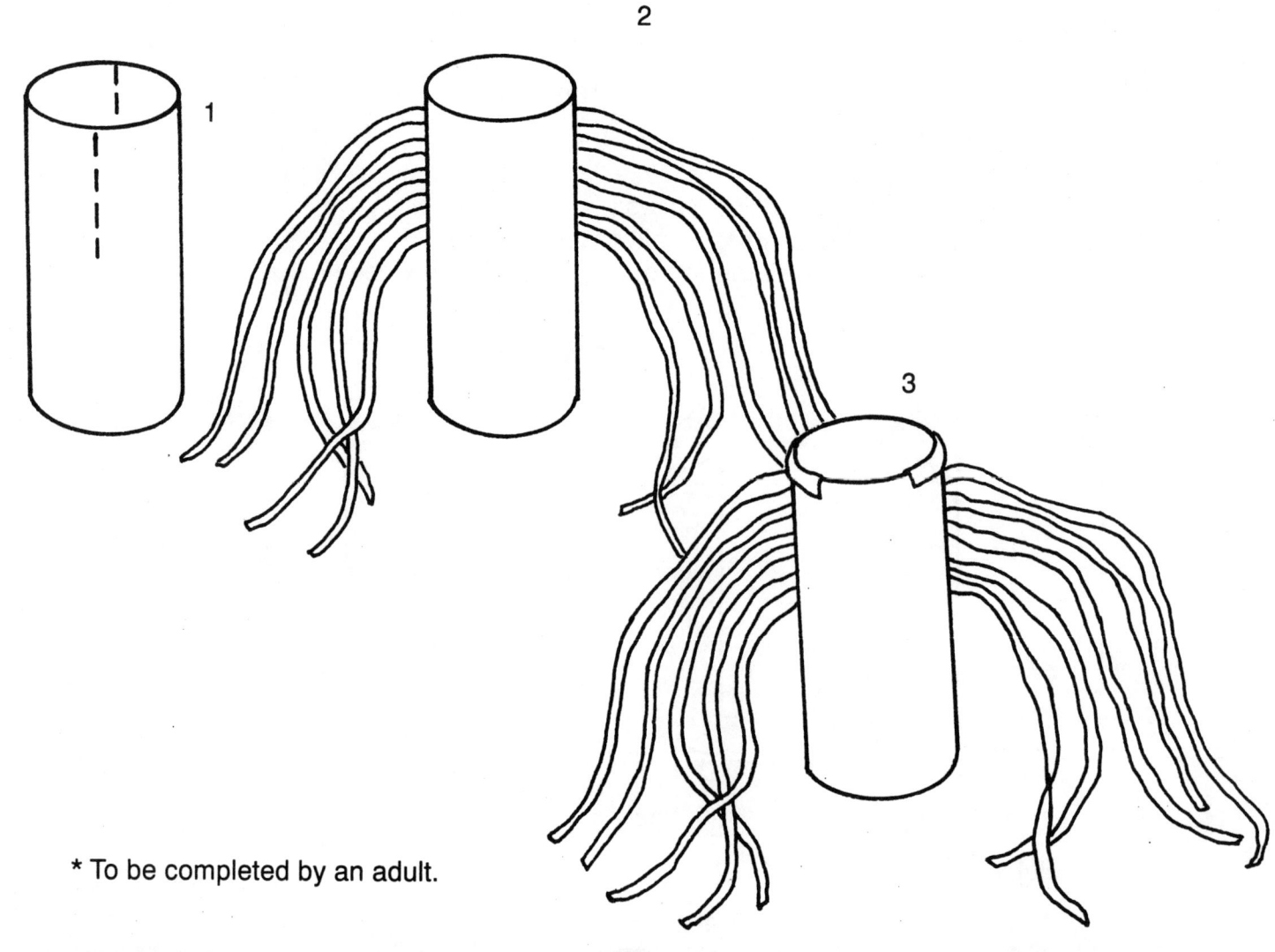

* To be completed by an adult.

BUTTERFLY

The butterfly is a symbol of new life. The butterfly breaks out of the cocoon changed from the caterpillar that entered it. Similarly, Christ left the tomb transformed from the body that was placed there.

MATERIALS:
Paper tube
Black paint and brush
Wing pattern, page 40
Construction paper
Scissors
Tissue paper
Glue
2 black pipe cleaners

INSTRUCTIONS:
1. Paint the paper tube black. Allow it to dry.
2. Place the wing pattern on page 40 on folded construction paper, and cut it out. Unfold it for the wings (illustration 1).
3. Using the teardrop-shaped patterns as guides, cut openings in the wings (illustration 2). Cut teardrop shapes from tissue paper slightly larger than the openings in the wings. Glue the tissue paper over the openings on the back side of the butterfly.
4. Glue the tube to the center of the open wings on the front side of the butterfly.
5. Add pipe cleaner "feelers" by forcing two pipe cleaners through the top of the painted tube. Twist ends to hold in place (illustration 3).

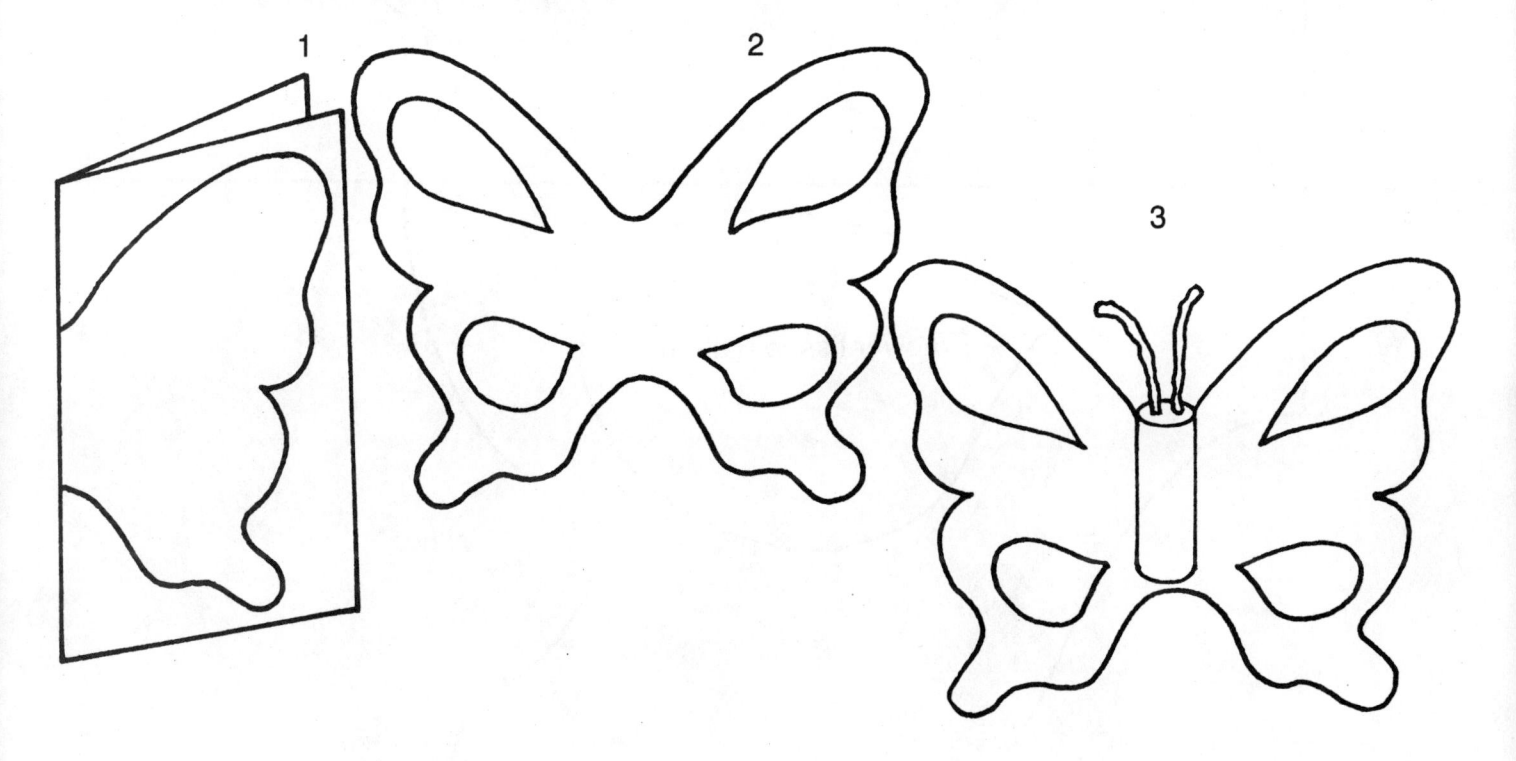

BUTTERFLY PATTERNS

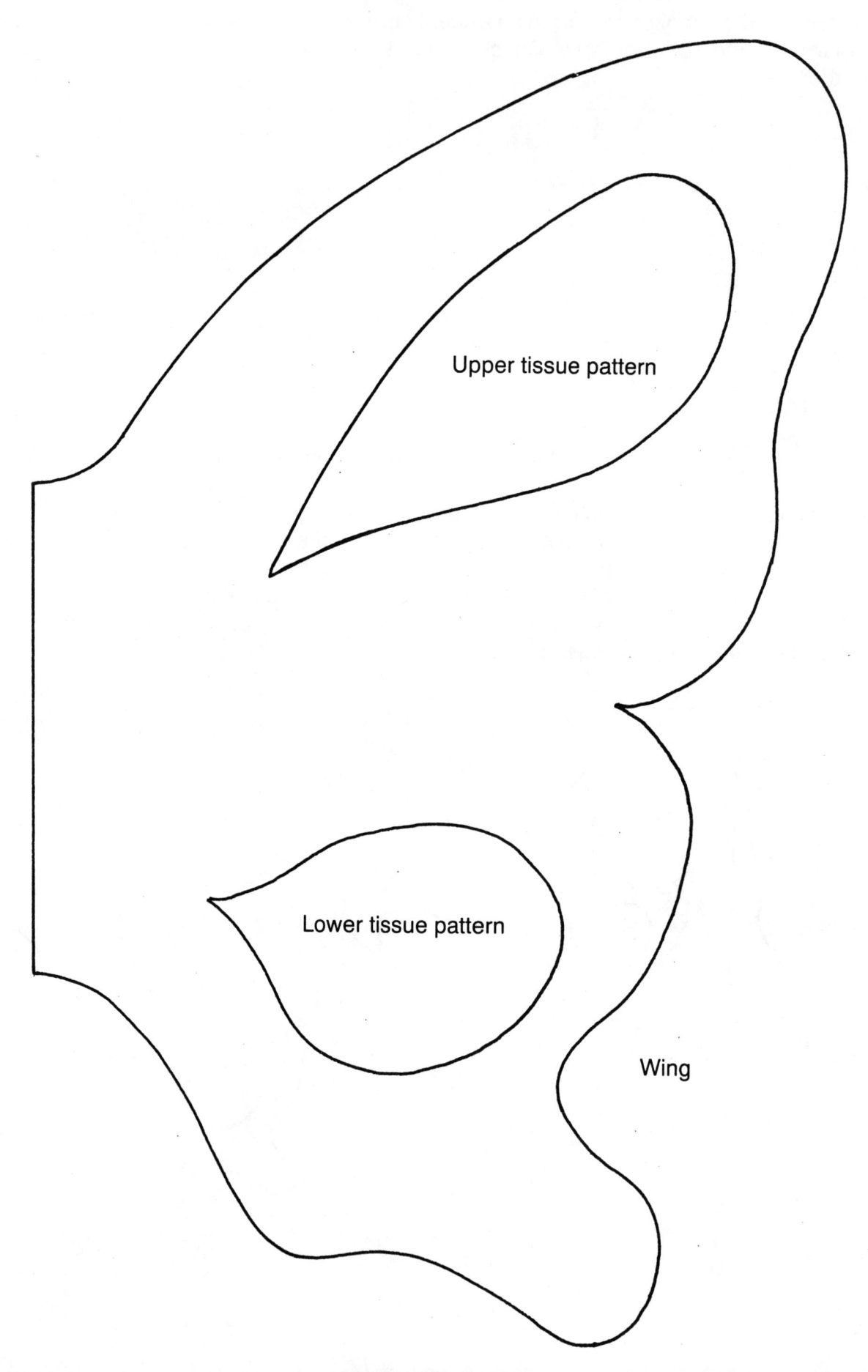

Upper tissue pattern

Lower tissue pattern

Wing

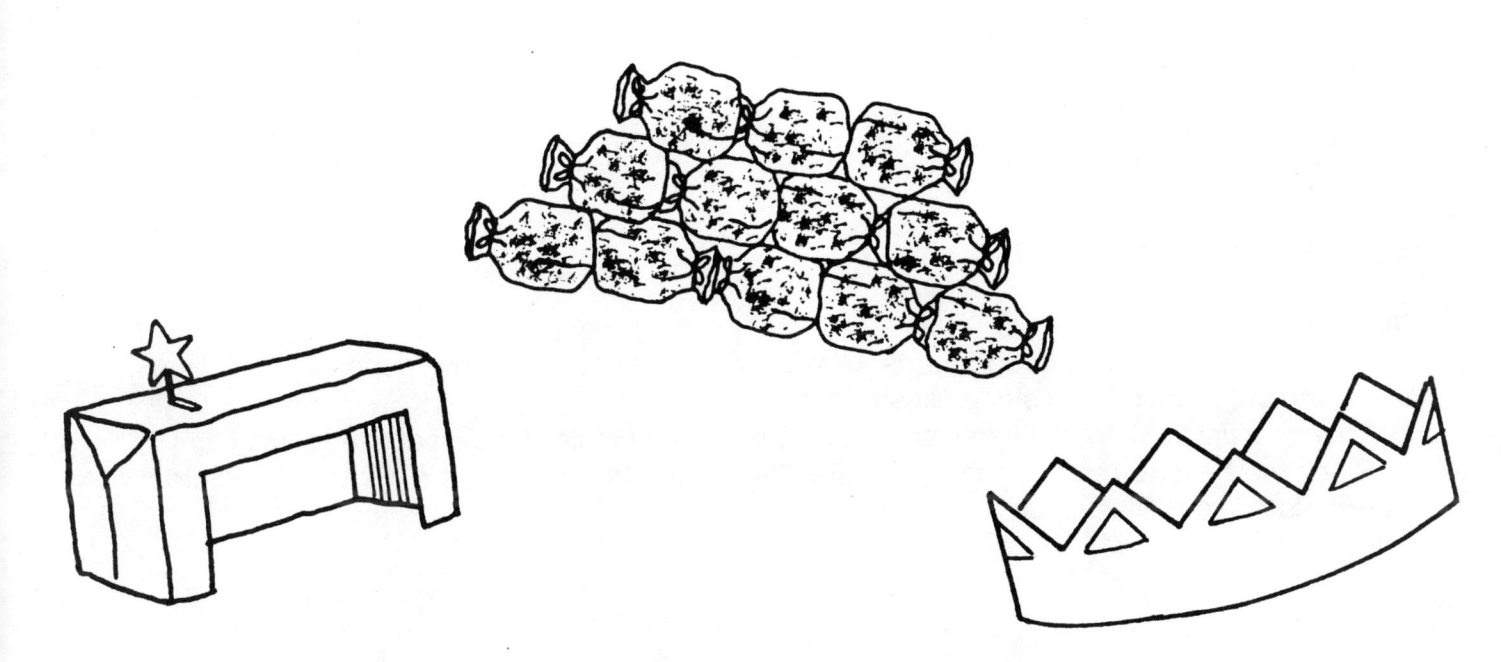

CRAFT IDEAS USING PAPER GROCERY BAGS

TWELVE STONES

"And tell them to take up twelve stones from the middle of Jordan."   Joshua 4:3a

MATERIALS:
Scissors
12 grocery bags
Newspaper
String
Sponges and paint (optional)

INSTRUCTIONS:
1. Stuff each grocery bag three-fourths full with crumpled sheets of newspaper.
2. Tie the bags closed with string (illustration 1).
3. Sponge paint the bags with gray and brown paint to resemble stones if desired (illustration 2).
4. Stack the bags to resemble the altar Israelites built after crossing the Jordan River into the Promised Land (illustration 3).

1   2    3

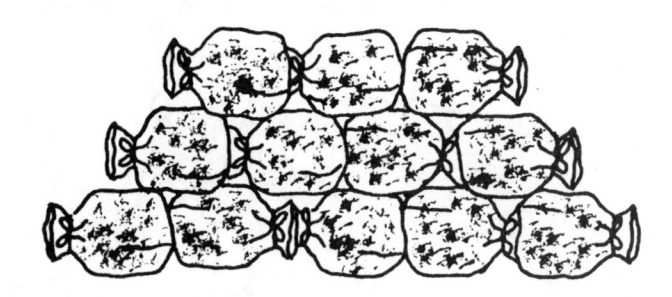

ADDITIONAL BIBLE REFERENCES:
Tower of Babel (Genesis 11:1-9)
Jacob's Memorial (Genesis 28:16-22)
Moses' Hands Grow Tired (Exodus 17:10-16)
Defeat of Jericho (Joshua 6)

TEN COMMANDMENTS

"And he wrote on the tablets the words of the covenant–the Ten Commandments."

Exodus 34:28b

MATERIALS:
2 grocery bags
Scissors
Pencil
Marker
Newspaper
Stapler

INSTRUCTIONS:
1. Cut off the bottom end of each bag.
2. Lay bags flat and trace an arched tablet shape on each (illustration 1).
3. Cut out the tablets, cutting through both layers of the bag at one time, including the sides. Cut a second pair of tablets from the other bag. You will have four tablet-shaped pieces of grocery bag.
4. Any printing (such as the name of the grocery store) should be on the inside of the project. Print the first five of the commandments on one tablet shape and the next five on the second one (illustration 2). These are provided in simplified form on page 44.
5. Place one printed tablet on top of a plain one. Staple along both sides and around the curved top (illustration 3). Assemble the second pair of tablets the same way.
6. Crumple newspaper, and stuff it between the two layers of each tablet.
7. Staple each end closed.

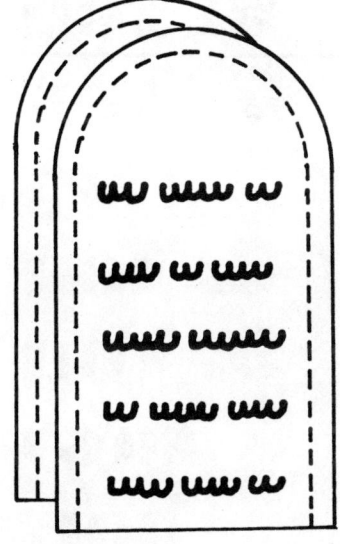

Shining Star Publications, Copyright © 1994

SS3805

1. You shall have no other gods before Me.
2. You shall not make an idol for yourself.
3. You shall not misuse the name of the Lord your God.
4. Remember the Sabbath day by keeping it holy.
5. Honor your father and your mother.

6. You shall not murder.
7. You shall not commit adultery.
8. You shall not steal.
9. You shall not give false testimony against your neighbor.
10. You shall not covet.

STABLE

"Because there was no room for them in the inn." Luke 2:7b

MATERIALS:
Grocery bag
Scissors
Yellow construction paper
Gold glitter
Glue
Straw or excelsior
Brad fastener (the longer the better)
4" x 6" index cards
Tape

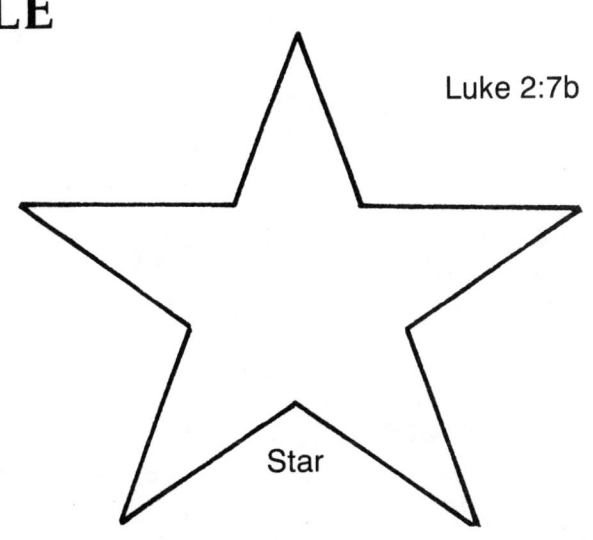

Star

INSTRUCTIONS:
1. Using the pattern on this page, cut a star from yellow construction paper. Glue glitter to the star; then allow it to dry.
2. Cut 10" off the grocery bag to save for another project (illustration 1). Make the stable from the bottom of the bag.
3. Cut a 9" x 6" rectangular opening on the side of the bag without any printing (illustration 2).
4. Glue one index card inside each end of the bag for reinforcement.
5. Set bag upside down, so the bottom can be the roof for the stable. Glue straw or excelsior around the bottom of the opening.
6. Push the brad fastener through the inside of the sack with metal pieces extending to the top. Bend down one piece. Tape the glittered star to the upright piece (illustration 3).
7. Place nativity figures (see pages 19-21) inside the stable.

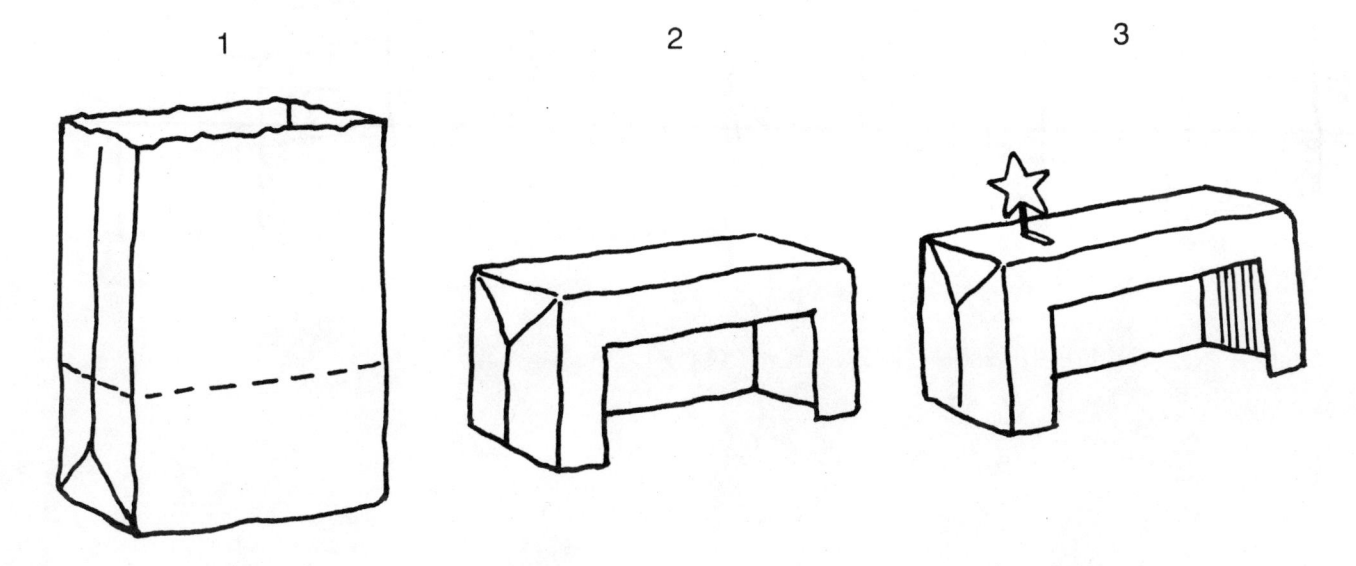

1   2   3

Shining Star Publications, Copyright © 1994   SS3805

BIBLE-TIME ROBE

"Now Israel loved Joseph more than any of his other sons . . . and he made a richly ornamented robe for him."

Genesis 37:3

MATERIALS:
Grocery bag
Scissors
Rolls of crepe paper
Glue

INSTRUCTIONS:
1. Cut a slit in the center of the grocery bag from the top to the middle of the folded bottom (illustration 1).
2. * Cut an oval in the bottom, large enough for a child's neck (illustration 2).
3. * Cut armholes in both sides of the bag.
4. Decorate the bag like a colorful robe by gluing strips of crepe paper to it (illustration 3).

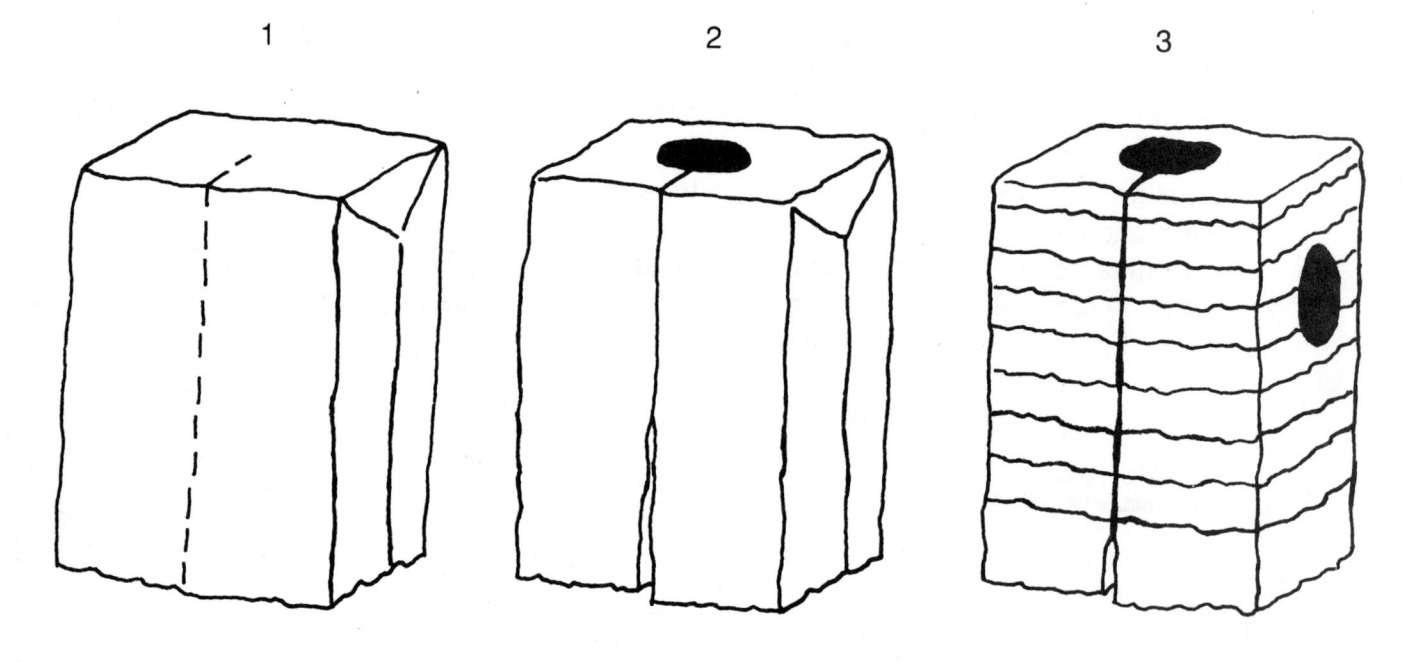

* May need to be completed by an adult.

ADDITIONAL BIBLE REFERENCES:
Samuel's Robe (1 Samuel 2:18-19)
Mordecai Honored (Esther 6)
Return of the Prodigal Son (Luke 15:20-24)

CROWN

"We do it to get a crown that will last forever." 1 Corinthians 9:25b

MATERIALS:
Scissors
Grocery bag
Tape
Glue
Markers
Buttons, aluminum foil, sequins (optional)

INSTRUCTIONS:
1. Cut strips from the grocery bag approximately 3" wide (illustration 1).
2. Fit a strip to child's head and tape the ends together.
3. Cut a series of 1" triangles along the top edge of the strip (illustration 2).
4. Color the triangle cutouts with markers. (Use the rest of the grocery bag as a mat to color on, so no colors get on the table.) Glue the colored triangles inside the crown points (illustration 3).
5. Add buttons, bits of aluminum foil, or sequins to decorate the crown.

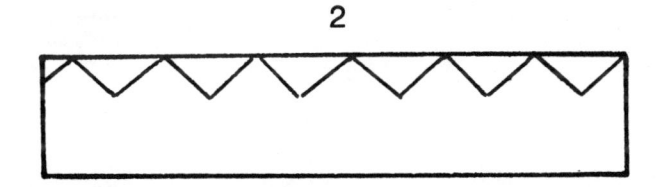

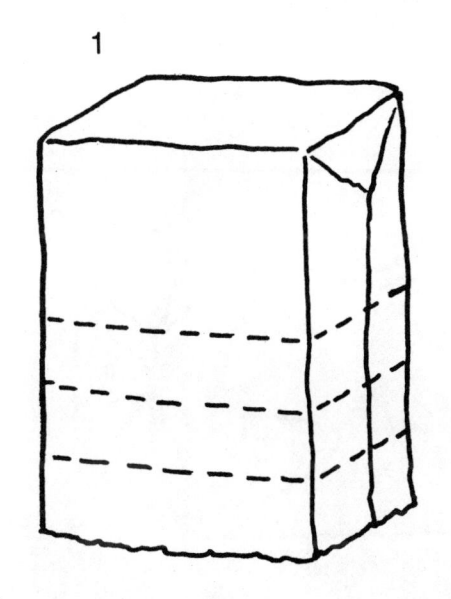

ADDITIONAL BIBLE REFERENCES:
King David (2 Samuel 5:1-5)
Queen Esther (Esther 2:1-18)
King Nebuchadnezzar (Daniel 3)
King Herod (Matthew 2:1-12)

FISH

"They caught such a large number of fish that their nets began to break."   Luke 5:6b

MATERIALS:
Grocery bag
Markers
Masking tape
Newspaper
String or yarn

INSTRUCTIONS:
1. With the bag flat, fold the bottom corners to the center. Tape in place. The tape may be applied in a decorative manner so that it adds to the overall design (illustration 1).
2. Draw an eye on each side of the bag near the pointed end. Add colors, fins, and gills to the bag with the markers (illustration 2).
3. Crumple single sheets of newspaper and stuff inside the bag.
4. Tie the tail of the fish with a piece of string or yarn about 3" from the end (illustration 3).

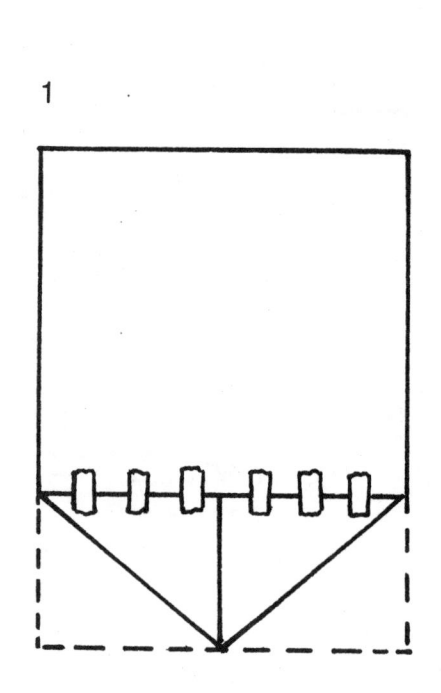

ADDITIONAL BIBLE REFERENCES:
Creation (Genesis 1:20-23)
Jonah (Jonah 1:17)
Feeding the Multitude (Matthew 14:13-21)
Appearance of the Resurrected Christ (Luke 24:36-44)

LOVE BANNER

"By this all men will know that you are my disciples, if you love one another." John 13:35

MATERIALS:
Iron (optional)
Grocery bag
Scissors
Masking tape
Damp sponge
Thin tempera paint
Construction paper
Glue
18" dowel rod
Yarn

INSTRUCTIONS:
1. Cut open the grocery bag and cut off the bottom (illustration 1).
2. Cut a large triangle from one end of the bag (illustration 2).
3. Make a 1 1/2" fold across the top. Tape with masking tape, leaving a space open to slide in the dowel rod.
4. Crumple the entire grocery bag, then smooth it out with your hand. *(An adult may press it with a cool iron.) Dip one end of the damp sponge into the paint. With very little paint in the sponge, rub it over the entire surface of the bag. The wrinkles in the bag should not take the paint, giving the bag a textured look.
5. Cut block letters from construction paper to spell out a short Bible verse or part of a verse, such as "Love God" or "Love One Another." Glue the letters on the bag.
6. Insert the dowel rod in the fold at the top. Tie a 24" piece of yarn to each end of the rod for hanging (illustration 3).

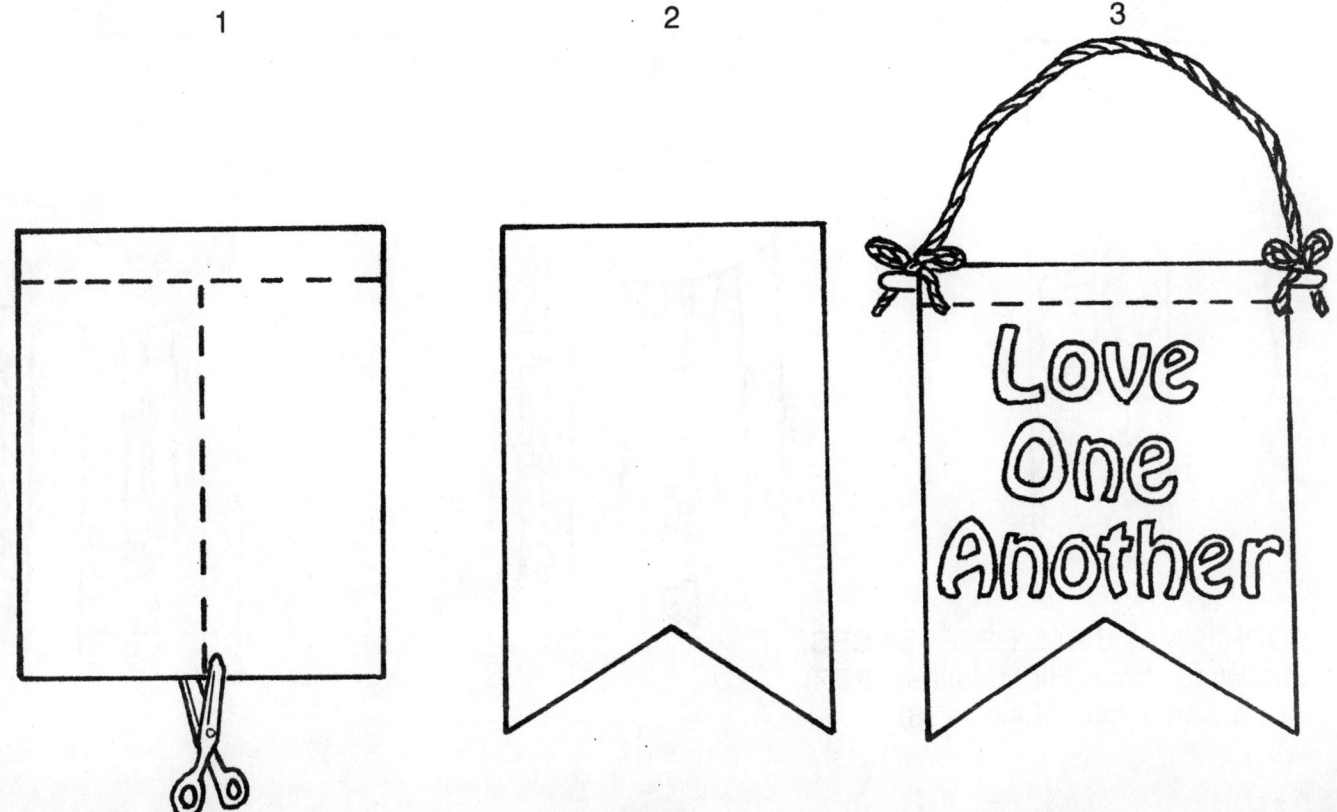

WIND SOCK

"Suddenly a sound like the blowing of a violent wind came from heaven."   Acts 2:2a

MATERIALS:
Grocery bag
Scissors
Newspaper
Crepe paper streamers (different colors)
Spray bottle filled with water
Tape
String
Bells
Hole punch

INSTRUCTIONS:
1. Cut a 4" x 16" strip from the grocery bag.
2. Cover the table with newspaper. Tear pieces of different colors of crepe paper and lay them on the grocery bag strip (illustration 1). Spray the crepe paper with water, and allow the colors to bleed through on the bag. Discard the wet crepe paper and allow the bag to dry.
3. Tape 15" pieces of crepe paper streamers to the plain side of the strip.
4. Cut four pieces of string each approximately 15" in length. Tie three bells on each string.
5. Tape the strings of bells between the crepe paper streamers.
6. Tape the two ends of the grocery bag strip together (illustration 2).
7. Punch three holes near the top edge of the strip. Tie a piece of string, 16" long, to each hole. Tie the three loose ends together. Tie a longer piece of string to the three for hanging (illustration 3).
8. Hang by an open window. Materials are not suitable for hanging outdoors.

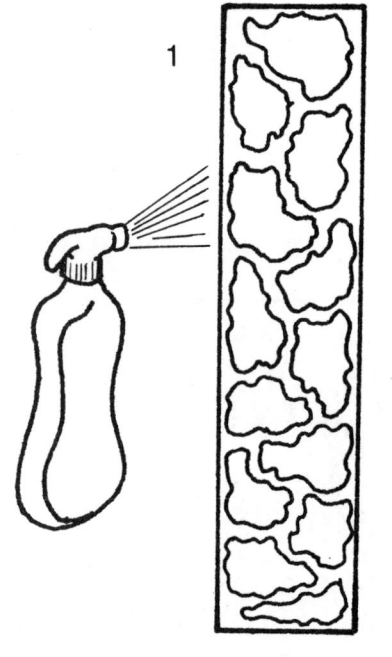

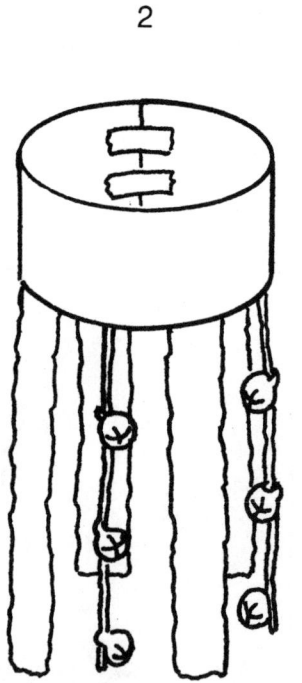

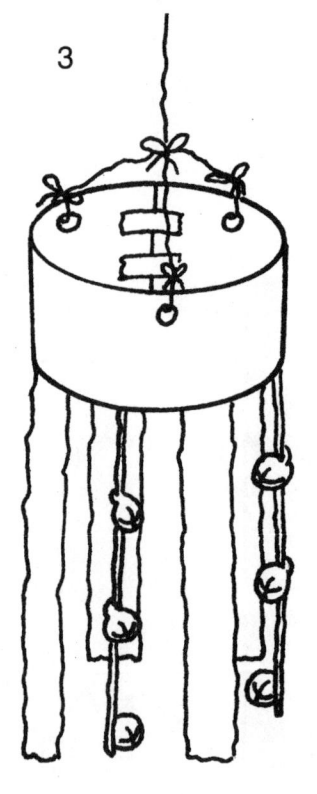

ADDITIONAL BIBLE REFERENCES:
The Wind Obeys Him (Matthew 8:27)
Being Born Again (John 3:7-8)

CRAFT IDEAS USING POLYSTYRENE TRAYS

EAGLE

"But those who hope in the Lord will renew their strength. They will soar on wings like eagles. . . ."
Isaiah 40:31

MATERIALS:
Craft knife
Rectangular polystyrene tray
Eagle patterns, page 54
Ink pen
Paper clip

INSTRUCTIONS:
1. Trace the eagle patterns on page 54 on a polystyrene tray (illustration 1). * Cut out the pieces.
2. Cut a slit where the wing should be inserted (illustration 2). Slide the wing through the body.
3. Attach the paper clip to the eagle's beak.
4. Throw it like a paper airplane and watch the eagle fly (illustration 3)!

* To be completed by an adult.

JESUS CALLED THE LITTLE CHILDREN

"Let the little children come to me, and do not hinder them, for the kingdom of God belongs to such as these."
Luke 18:16b

MATERIALS:
Craft knife
Polystyrene tray
Jesus and children patterns, page 54
Tagboard
Glue
Scissors
Crayons
Craft stick
Tape

INSTRUCTIONS:
1. Reproduce the figures of Jesus, the tab, and the children on page 54. Glue each to the tagboard.
2. Color the figures; then cut them out. Cut out the tab and fold it in half.
3. Tape the figure of children to the end of a craft stick (illustration 1).
4. Tape one end of the paper tab to the back of the figure of Jesus, and tape the other end of the tab to the tray (illustration 2).
5. * Cut a slit in the meat tray using a craft knife. Insert the stick through the slot (illustration 3). Move the children towards Jesus.

* To be completed by an adult.

JESUS AND CHILDREN PATTERNS

EAGLE PATTERNS

FOUR SEASONS MOBILE

"There is a time for everything, and a season for every activity under heaven."

Ecclesiastes 3:1

MATERIALS:
Polystyrene tray
Pencil
Season patterns, page 56
Crayons, markers, or watercolors
Scissors
Yarn
Tape

INSTRUCTIONS:
1. Copy the season patterns on page 56. Color them, and cut them out.
2. Punch a hole near each corner of the tray. Punch another hole in the center (illustration 1).
3. Cut four pieces of yarn about 18" long and one 10" long.
4. Thread the shorter piece of yarn through the middle hole, and tie a knot on the bottom. Thread the remaining pieces of yarn, one through each corner hole, and tie a knot on the top (illustration 2).
5. Tape the seasonal figures along the yarn using a separate season for each piece of yarn (illustration 3).

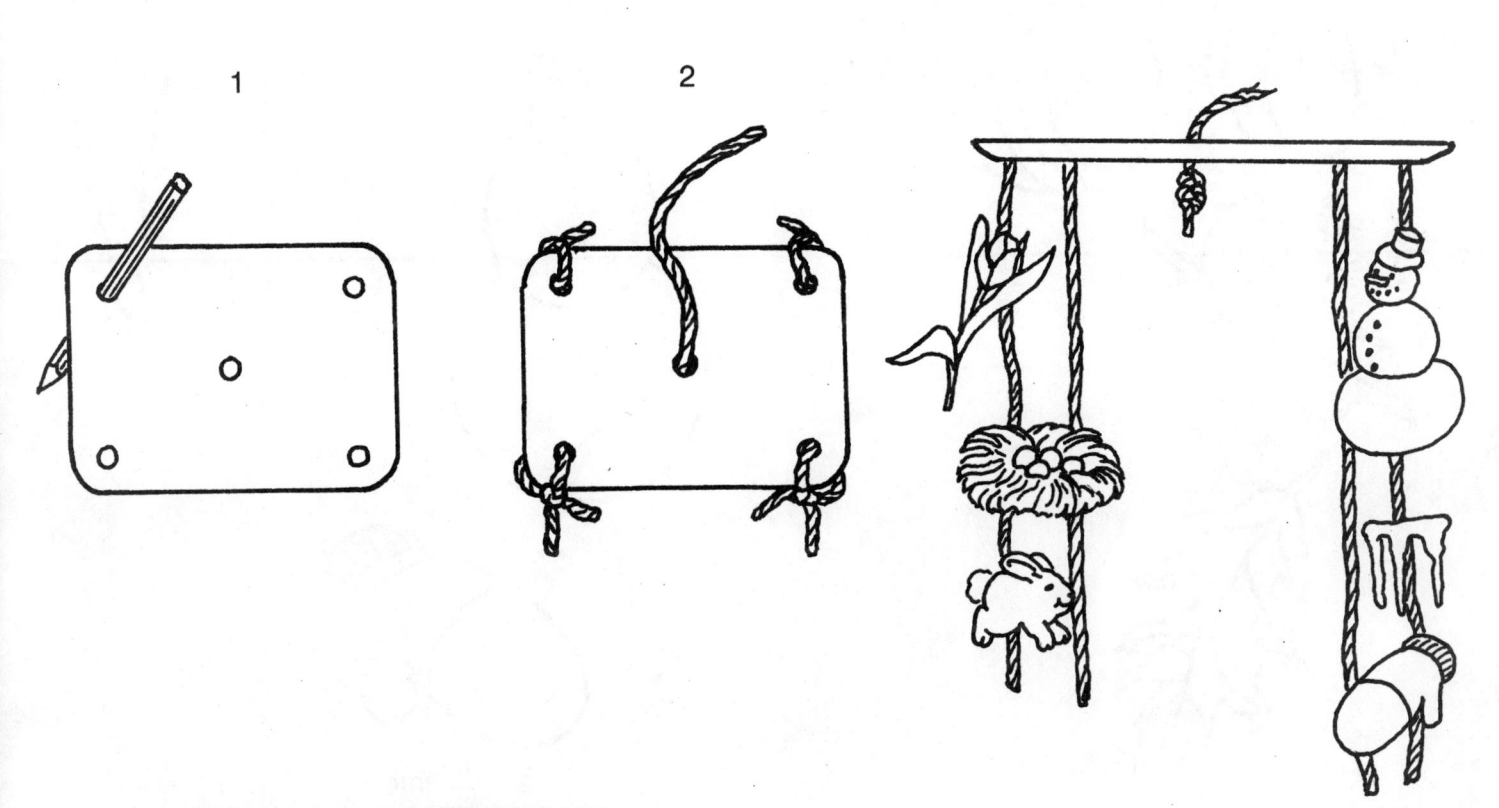

ADDITIONAL BIBLE REFERENCES:
Creation (Genesis 1:14)
Daniel Praises God (Daniel 2:20-23)
Paul Credits God for Seasons (Acts 14:15b-17)

SEASON PATTERNS

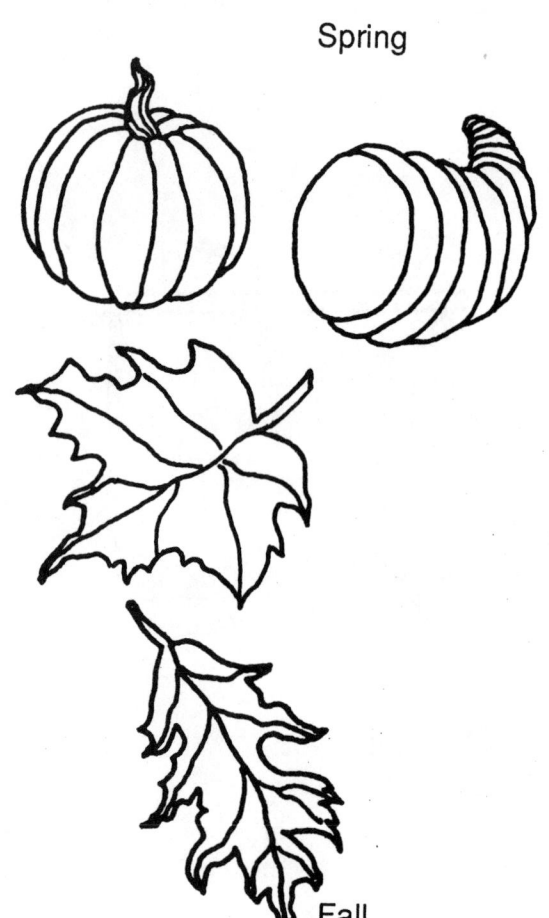

Spring

Summer

Fall

Winter

56

MEMORY VERSE FRAME

"The word is very near you; it is in your mouth and in your heart so you may obey it."

Deuteronomy 30:14

MATERIALS:
Sturdy scissors
Cardboard milk carton
Polystyrene tray
Paper
Markers
Glitter
Glue
Tape

INSTRUCTIONS:
1. * Cut the top off the milk carton so only 2 1/2" sides remain (illustration 1).
2. * Use the illustration as a guide to cut the base of the milk carton into an easel (illustration 2). Cut approximately 1 1/2" from right corner on a diagonal to bottom right corner approximately 1/4" from bottom of carton. Cut opposite side in same manner. Finish front of easel by cutting off excess, forming a triangular point.
3. Glue glitter in a decorative pattern around the inside edges of the tray.
4. Cut piece of paper smaller than the frame. Choose a Bible verse you would like to memorize. Print it on the paper. Tape the Bible verse to the center of the tray (illustration 3). Verses may be changed weekly.

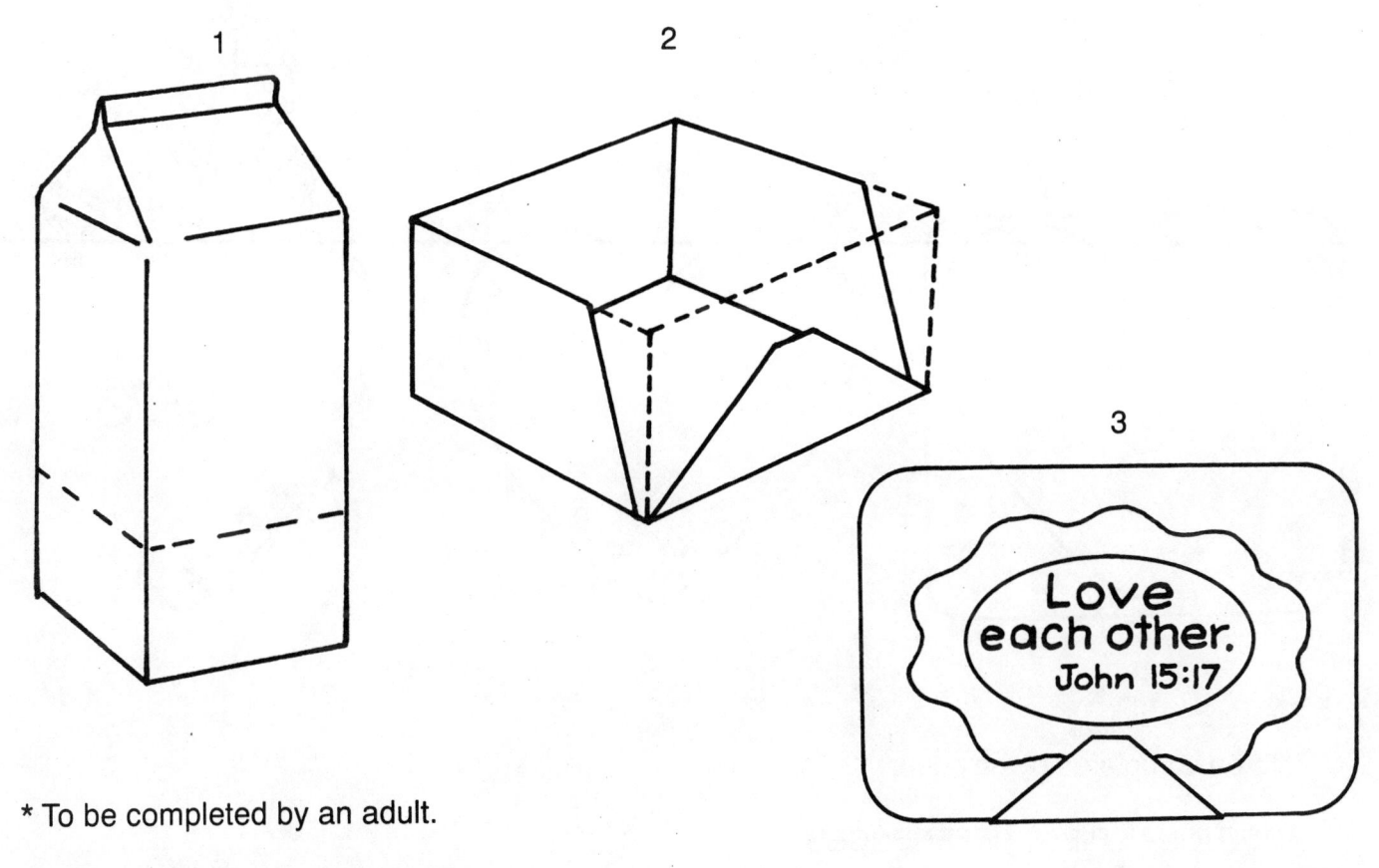

* To be completed by an adult.

ADDITIONAL BIBLE REFERENCE:
Keeping God's Commands (Proverbs 3:1)

LOVE PLAQUE

"This is [Christ's] command: 'Love each other.'" John 15:17

MATERIALS:
Sturdy scissors
Nail
2 large polystyrene trays (same size)
Permanent marker
Yarn
Transparent tape
Silk flowers

INSTRUCTIONS:
1. * Cut two identical hearts, one from each tray (illustration 1).
2. * Place one heart on top of the other. Use the nail to punch holes at 1" intervals near the edge of the hearts (illustration 2). Punch two holes at the top for hanging.
3. Print the word LOVE in the center of one heart.
4. Stiffen one end of a piece of yarn by wrapping it with tape. Tie the other end of the yarn through both holes starting at one side. Stitch the two hearts together and tie a knot at the end. With the excess yarn, form a loop for hanging (illustration 3).
5. Put flowers inside.

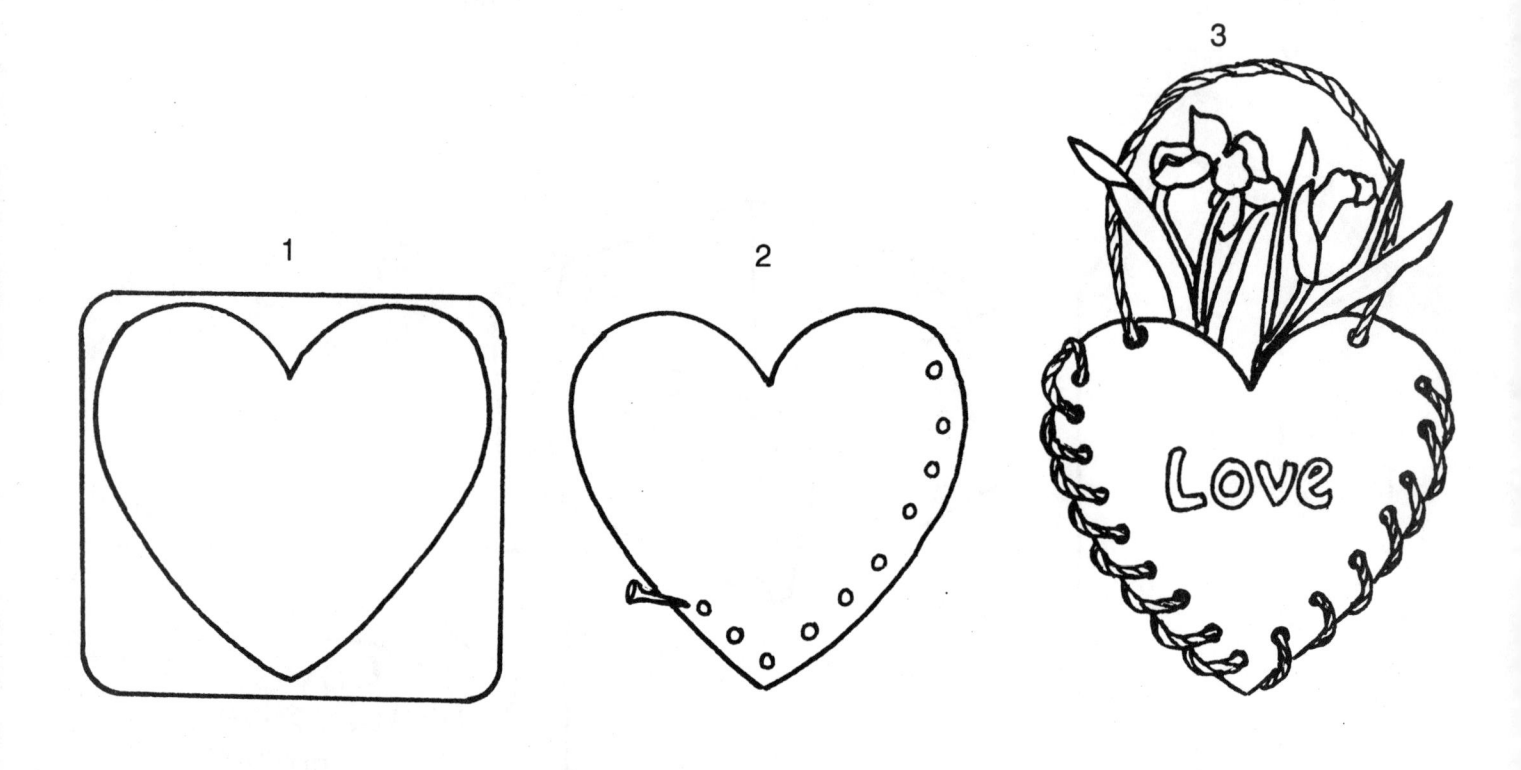

* To be completed by an adult.

ADDITIONAL BIBLE REFERENCES:
Loving God (Deuteronomy 6:5)
Love Means Obeying (John 14:15)

THANKSGIVING WALL HANGING

". . . let us be thankful . . . ." Hebrews 12:28

MATERIALS:
3 polystyrene trays (same size)
Scissors
Pencil
60" of yarn
Paper
Crayons
Glue
Ribbon, trim, rickrack, etc.
Nail
Transparent tape

INSTRUCTIONS:
1. Cut three pieces of paper to fit inside the trays.
2. * Use the nail to carefully punch two holes near the top of each tray and two holes near the bottom (illustration 1).
3. On one piece of paper print the Bible message "Let us be thankful."
4. Use two pieces of paper to draw pictures of things for which we are thankful.
5. Glue one piece of paper to each tray. Add ribbon, trim, or rickrack (illustration 2).
6. Tie a knot in one end of the yarn. Stiffen other end of yarn by wrapping it with tape. Bring the yarn from the back of one tray and thread the yarn through the hole on the left side of each tray. Place the tray with the Bible verse on top. Leave extra yarn at the top for hanging. Thread the yarn through all the holes on the right side (illustration 3).

* To be completed by an adult.

STAR OF DAVID

The six-pointed star is a symbol of Judaism. It reminds us of our Judeo-Christian heritage.

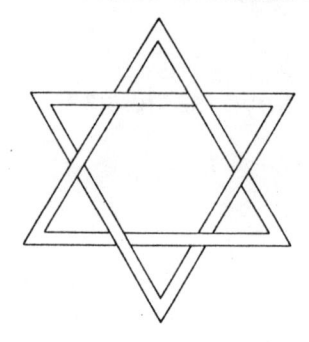

MATERIALS:
Nail
Polystyrene tray
Star of David pattern
70" of yarn
Tape

INSTRUCTIONS:
1. Copy the star pattern on this page (enlarging or reducing to fit tray). Cut it out and tape it in the center of the tray.
2. * Use the nail to carefully punch a hole at each of the six points (illustration 1).
3. Remove the star pattern. Number the holes as shown in illustration 2. Stiffen one end of the yarn by wrapping it with tape. Thread the yarn through hole number one, and tie a large enough knot on the back side to keep the yarn in place.
4. Make the Star of David pattern by sewing the lines of one triangle first (illustration 2). Then sew the other triangle (illustration 3). The star is easy to make but difficult to sew. You will have to go through each hole more than once to make each line.

Example: 1 → 3 (front side)
3 → 5 (back side)
5 → 1 (front side)
1 → 3 (back side)
3 → 5 (front side), etc.

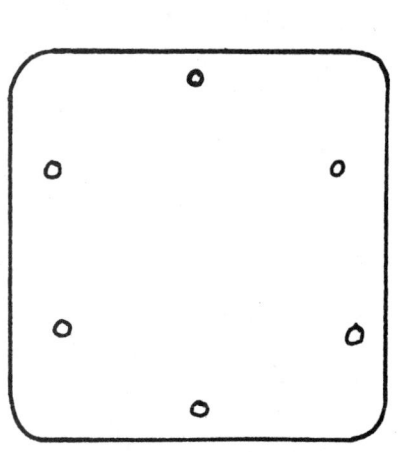

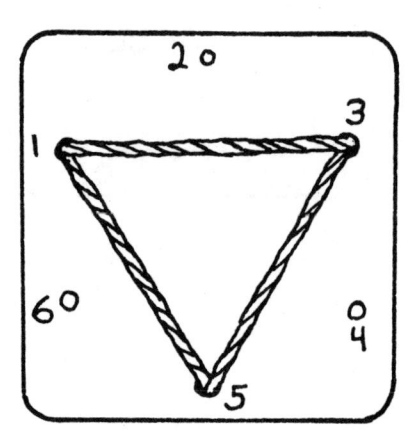

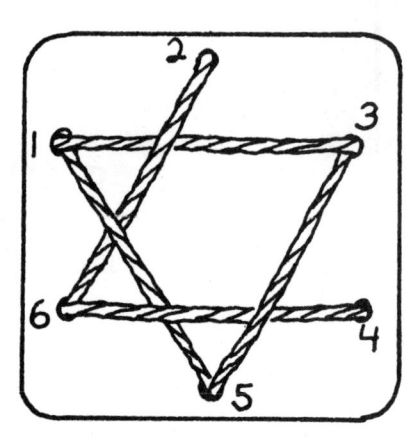

* To be completed by an adult.

CRAFT IDEAS USING CARDBOARD MILK CARTONS

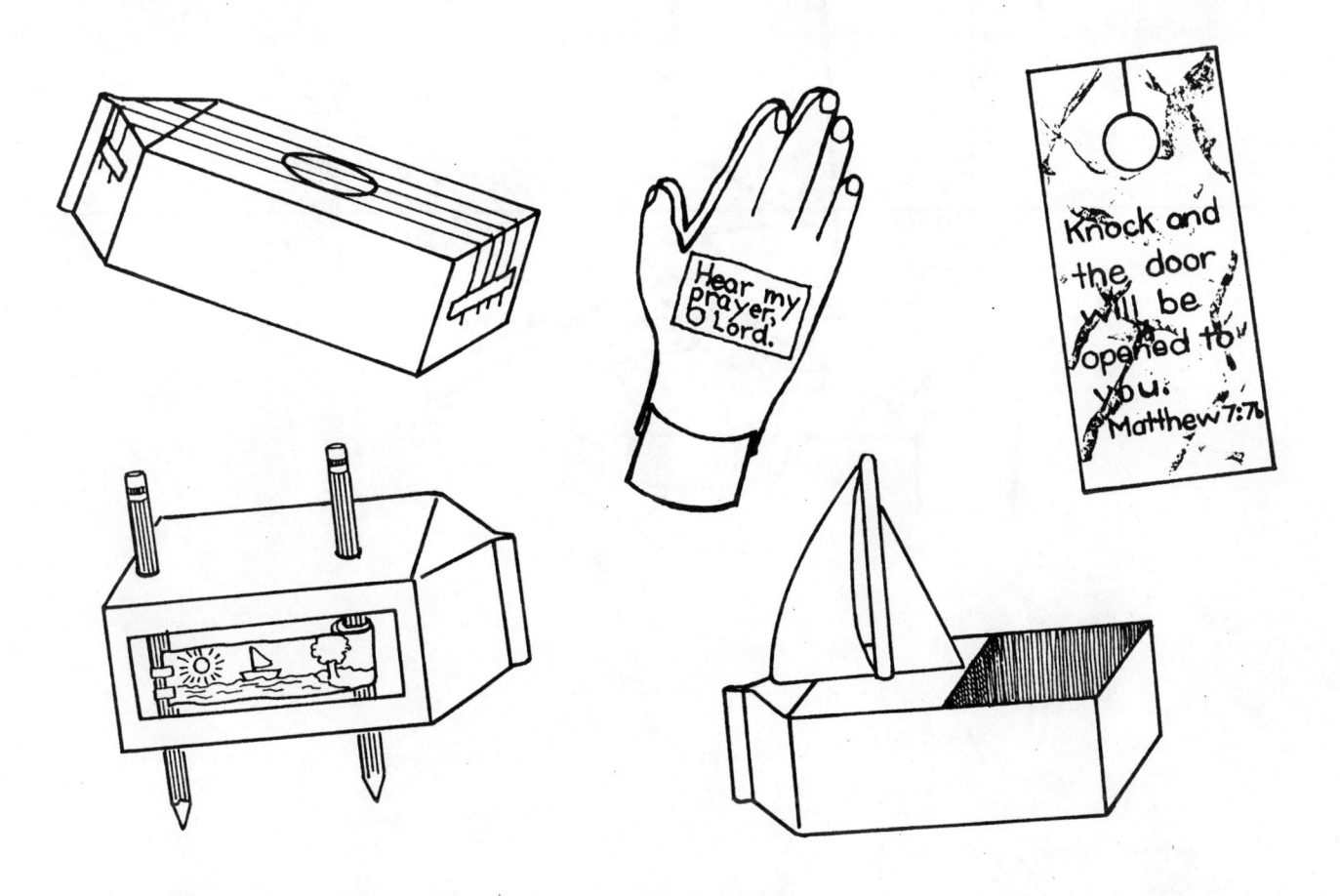

GENERAL INSTRUCTIONS FOR WORKING WITH MILK CARTONS

Each project on the following pages uses a half-gallon size milk or juice carton. Be sure the carton has been washed and is completely dry before beginning.

For some projects, the milk cartons need to be glued back into their original, unopened form. * A glue gun works well, but extreme caution must be exercised when using it around children. Thick, white craft glue also works, but takes longer to dry. If using white glue, a clip-type clothespin will hold the carton closed until the glue is dry. Any cutting on a cardboard carton should be done by an adult.

The cartons may be spray painted with enamel paint. Be sure to spray in a well-ventilated room or outside on a calm day. Cover the entire work area with newspaper before beginning. Plan to give the carton two or three light coats to prevent running. Colored construction paper, fabric, or felt may also be glued to the outside of the carton to cover the printing. See page 6 for additional suggestions of ways to decorate the cartons.

* To be completed by an adult.

DOORKNOB HANGER

"But as for me and my household, we will serve the Lord." Joshua 24:15b

MATERIALS:
Sturdy scissors
Cardboard milk carton
Light colored construction paper
2 colors of tempera paint
2 margarine tubs
2 marbles
2 spoons
Square cake pan
Glue
Black fine-tip marker

INSTRUCTIONS:
1. Cut the construction paper into a rectangle the same size as one side of the milk carton, approximately 3 3/4" by 7 1/2".
2. Place the construction paper in a cake pan. Choose two complementary colors of paint; put one color of paint in each margarine tub. Place a marble in each margarine tub. Spoon each paint-covered marble into the cake pan. Tilt the pan so that the marble rolls across the construction paper and leaves a trail of paint. Remove the paper from the pan and allow it to dry.
3. * While the paint is drying, carefully cut the top and bottom off the milk carton and discard. Cut apart the four side panels, saving three sides for future projects.
4. Cut a 1" slit from the top of the rectangle. Cut a circle at the end of the slit that measures 1 1/2" in diameter (illustration 1, page 64).
5. Glue the marble-painted construction paper to the printed side of the milk carton panel (illustration 2, page 64). If the paint is still damp, carefully blot it with a paper towel. Cut the slit and circle in the construction paper to match the one in the milk carton panel.
6. Print the Bible verse and reference on the marble-painted construction paper (illustration 3, page 64).

* To be completed by an adult.

ADDITIONAL BIBLE REFERENCES:
Jesus at the Door (Revelation 3:20a)
Praying in Your Room (Matthew 6:6a)
The Open Door (Matthew 7:7)

DOORKNOB HANGER

1   2   3

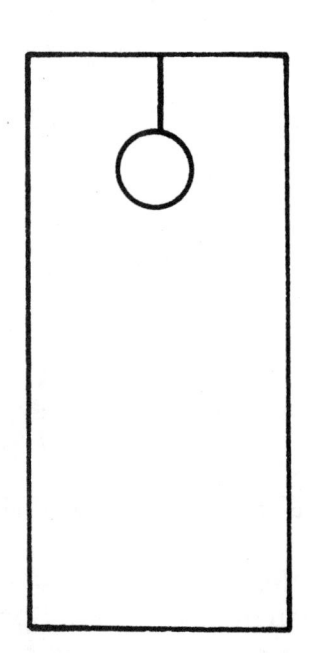

Knock and the door will be opened to you.
Matthew 7:7b

PRAYING HANDS PATTERN

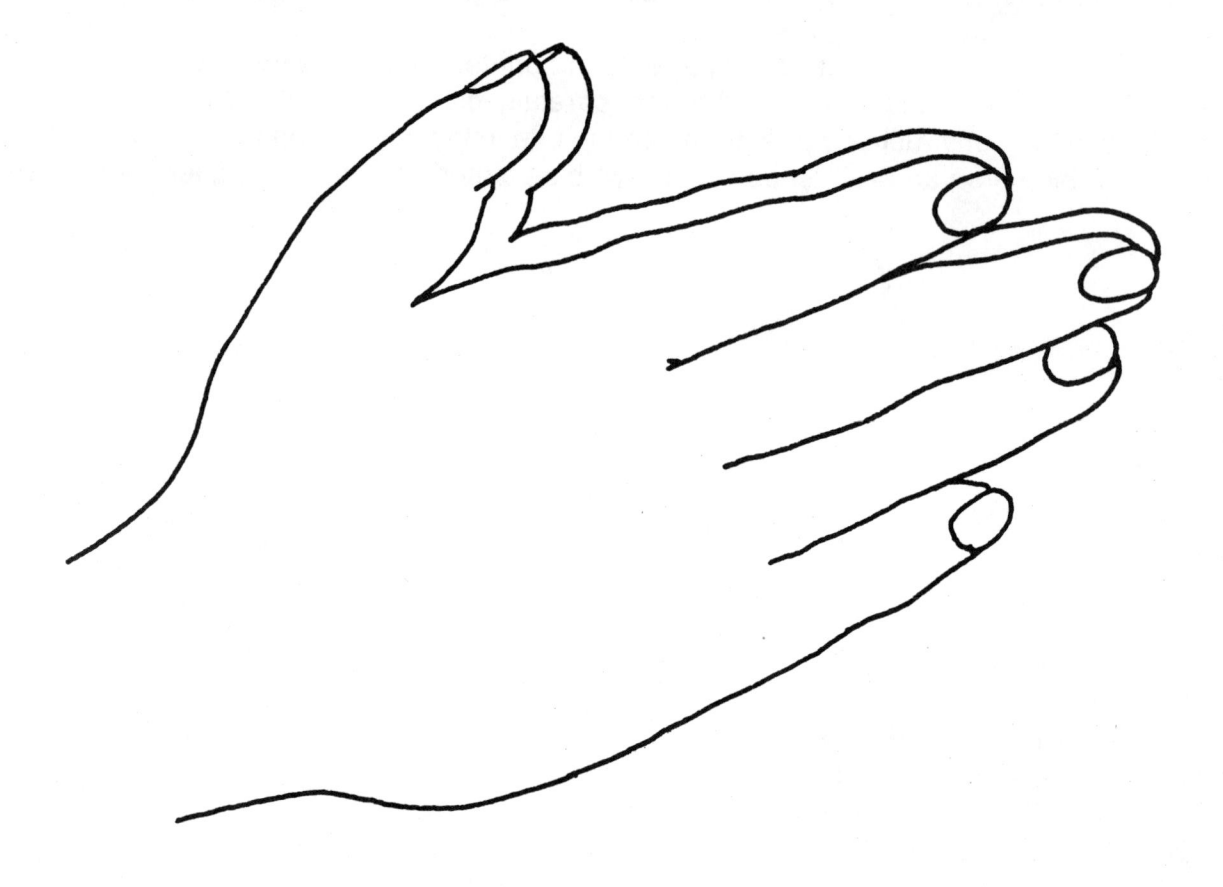

PRAYER REMINDER

"Hear my prayer, O Lord."   Psalm 39:12a

MATERIALS:
Sturdy scissors
Cardboard milk carton
Juice can
Construction paper
Praying hands pattern, page 64
Pink, tan, or brown construction paper
Printed prayer
Glue

INSTRUCTIONS:
1. * Cut the can to about 1 1/2" tall. Glue a 1 1/2" strip of construction paper around it.
2. Cut two 1/2" slits on opposite sides of the can (illustration 1).
3. * Cut the four side panels from the milk carton. Use one to cut the praying hands pattern (illustration 2).
4. Cut two sets of praying hands from construction paper. Glue the construction paper hands to both sides of the milk carton hands.
5. Copy the Lord's Prayer, or write your own prayer on paper that will fit on the praying hands. Glue the prayer in place. Put a second prayer on the other side if you like.
6. Slide the praying hands into the slots of the juice can (illustration 3). Set this craft on the dinner table or on a nightstand as a prayer reminder.

     1   2 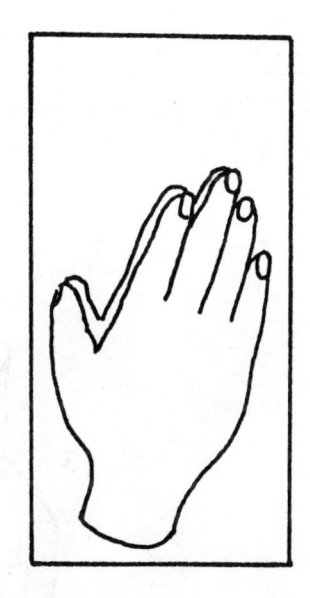   3

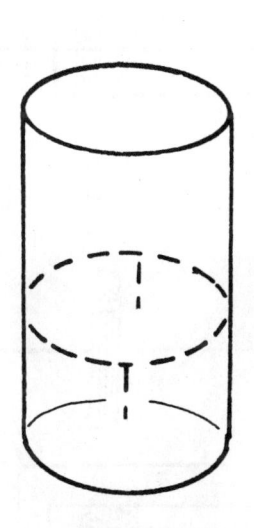

* To be completed by an adult.

ADDITIONAL BIBLE REFERENCES:
What to Pray About (Philippians 4:6)
The Lord's Prayer (Luke 11:1-4)

BIBLE STORY VIEWER

"I will perpetuate your memory through all generations." Psalm 45:17a

MATERIALS:
Scissors or craft knife
Cardboard milk carton
Roll of paper for a calculator
2 pencils or 6" dowel rods
Old Sunday school papers and glue or crayons
Tape
Large nail

INSTRUCTIONS:
1. Draw scenes from a Bible story on a long strip of calculator paper. If you prefer, cut pictures from Sunday school materials, and glue them in order on the strip of paper.
2. * Cut an opening from one side of the carton approximately 5" long (illustration 1).
3. Using the nail, punch two holes at either end of the opening. Stick pencils or dowels through these holes (illustration 2).
4. Reach through the opening to tape one end of the picture strip to each pencil (illustration 3). Roll the strip to the right pencil with the first scene visible in the opening.
5. Glue the milk carton opening closed.
6. Unroll the strip to retell the Bible story.

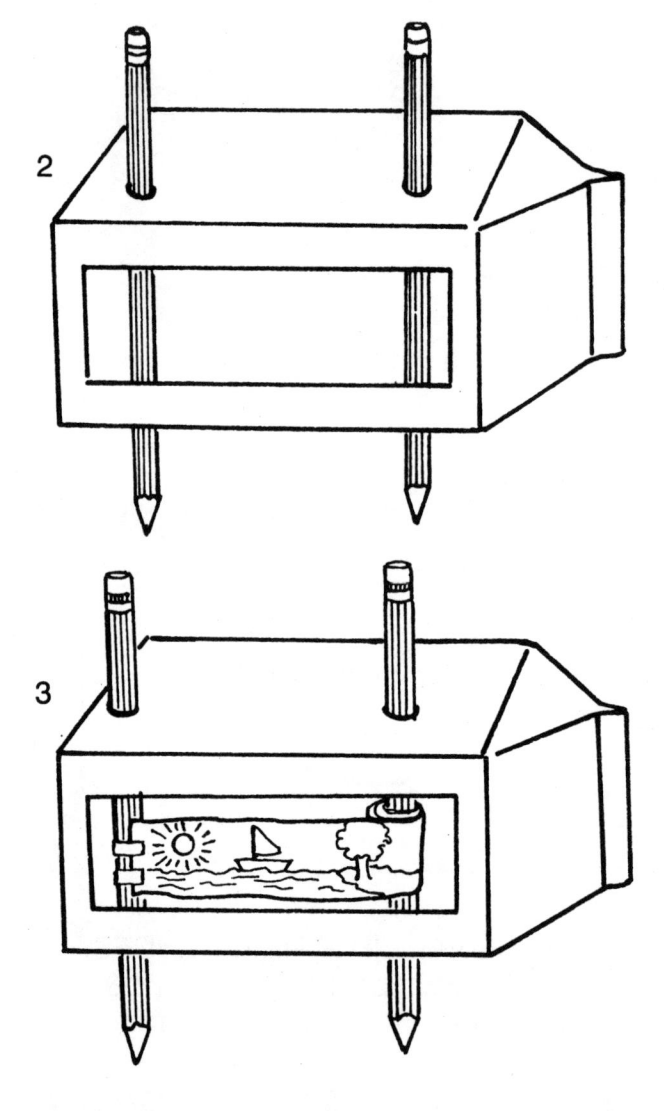

* To be completed by an adult.

BOAT

"He said, 'Throw your net on the right side of the boat and you will find some.' When they did, they were unable to haul the net in because of the large number of fish."   John 21:6

MATERIALS:
Scissors or craft knife
Brown spray paint
Cardboard milk carton
Glue
Wooden chopstick or 8" dowel
Sail patterns, page 68
White typing paper
Transparent tape
Large nail
Pencil

INSTRUCTIONS:
1. Glue the pouring spout of the carton closed.
2. * Cut out half of one side of the carton (illustration 1).
3. Using the nail, punch a hole into the other half of the carton. Push a chopstick or 8" dowel in the hole to make a mast. Glue in place if necessary (illustration 2).
4. * Paint the boat and "mast" with brown spray paint.
5. Use the patterns on page 68 to trace a sail on white paper. Cut them out, and tape to the mast (illustration 3).

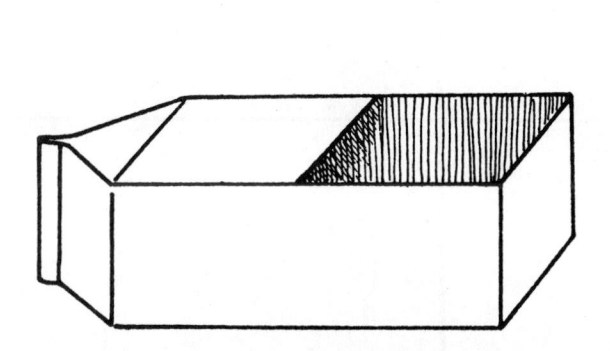

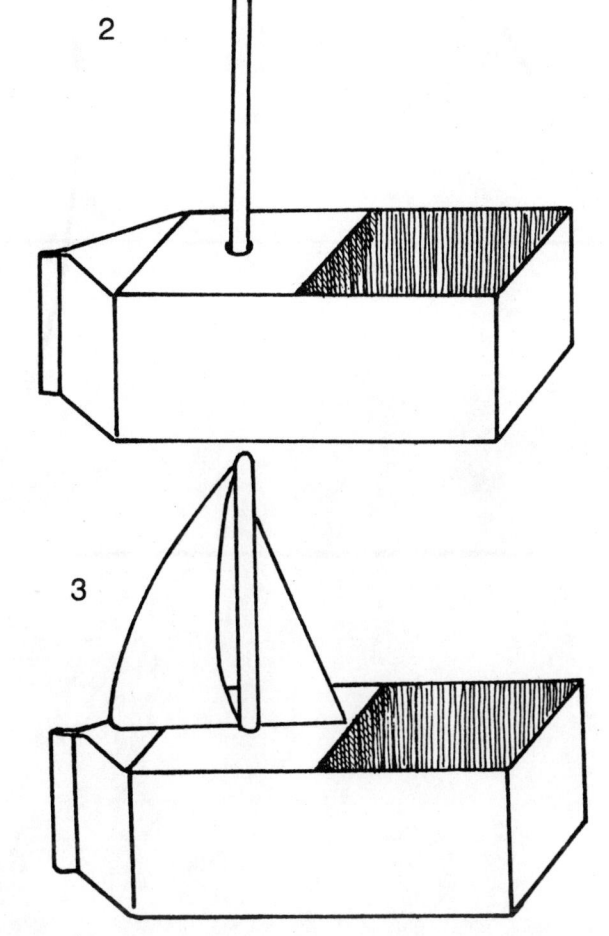

* To be completed by an adult.

ADDITIONAL BIBLE REFERENCES:
Calling the First Disciples (Mark 1:16-19)
Jesus Calms the Storm (Matthew 8:18, 23-27)
Jesus Walks on Water (Mark 6:45-51)

SAIL PATTERNS

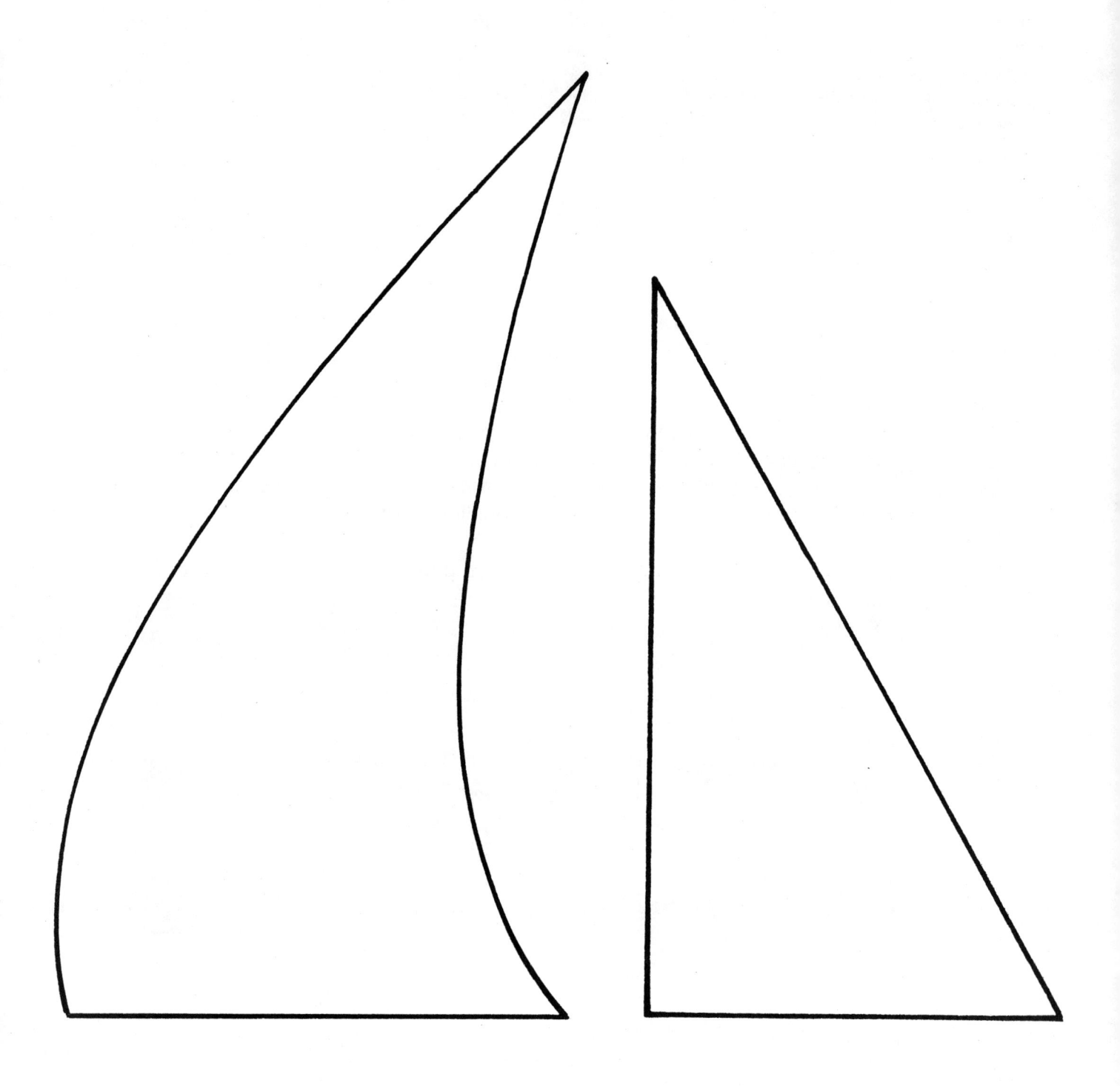

TALKING PUPPET

"Daniel answered, . . . 'My God sent his angel, and he shut the mouths of the lions.'"
Daniel 6:21-22a

MATERIALS:
Scissors or craft knife
Cardboard milk carton
Glue
Pink or red, tan or brown construction paper
Face patterns, pages 70-71
Markers or crayons
Yarn

INSTRUCTIONS:
1. * Cut the top off the milk carton so the sides measure approximately 3 1/2" (illustration 1).
2. * Cut away two opposing corners, leaving two triangular-shaped corners intact (illustration 2).
3. Glue a 3 3/4" square piece of pink or red construction paper to the bottom of the carton. This will become the puppet's mouth.
4. Score a diagonal line inside the carton. Fold the bottom back onto itself (illustration 3).
5. Trace the face patterns on pages 70 and 71 on construction paper. Cut the two pieces out, and lightly fold the face pieces in half. Glue the upper face to one corner of the milk carton and the lower face to the other. The construction paper will extend beyond the triangular corners of the carton.
6. Add yarn for hair and an appropriate construction paper headdress.

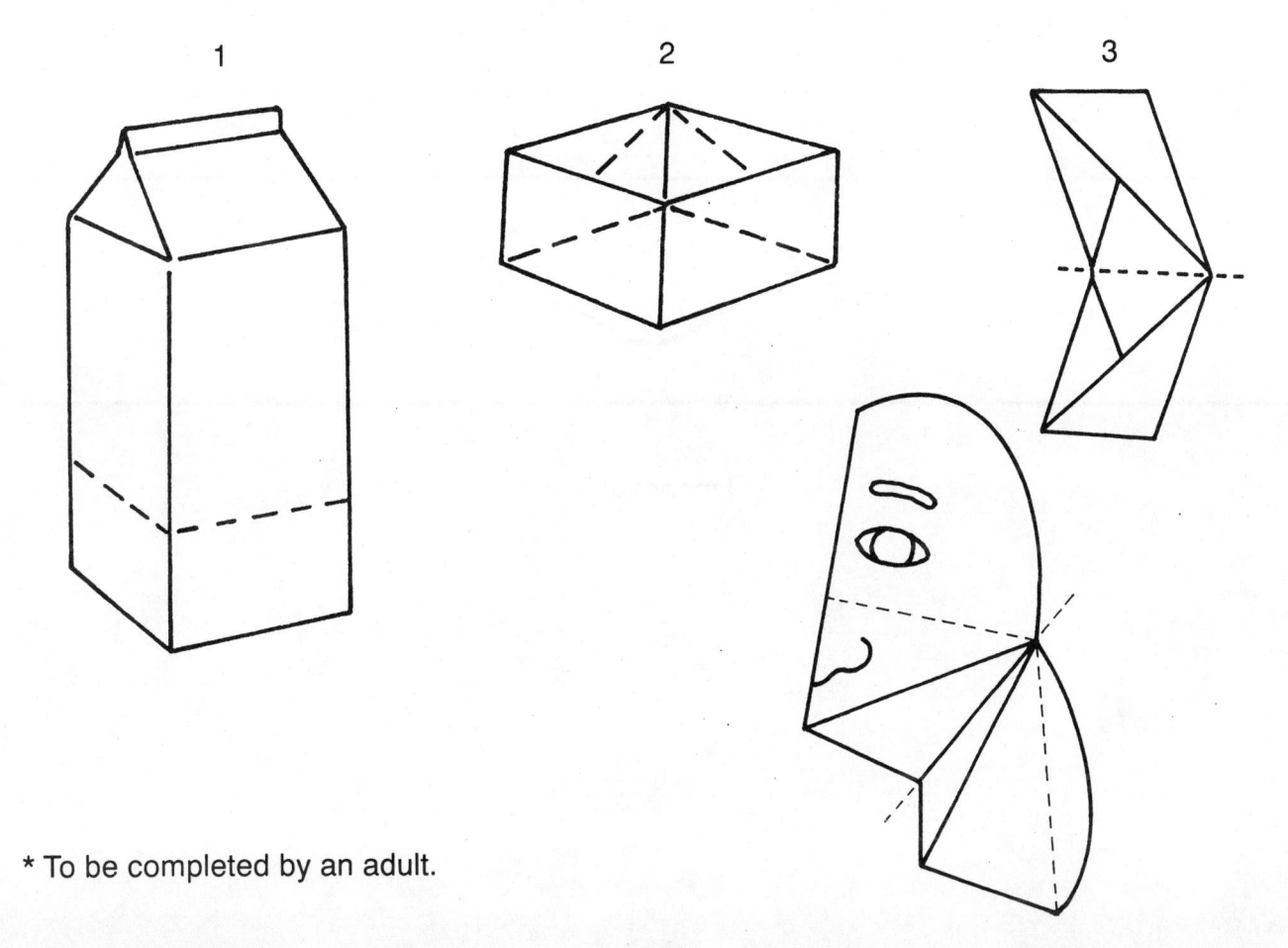

* To be completed by an adult.

PUPPET PATTERN

Upper face

PUPPET PATTERN

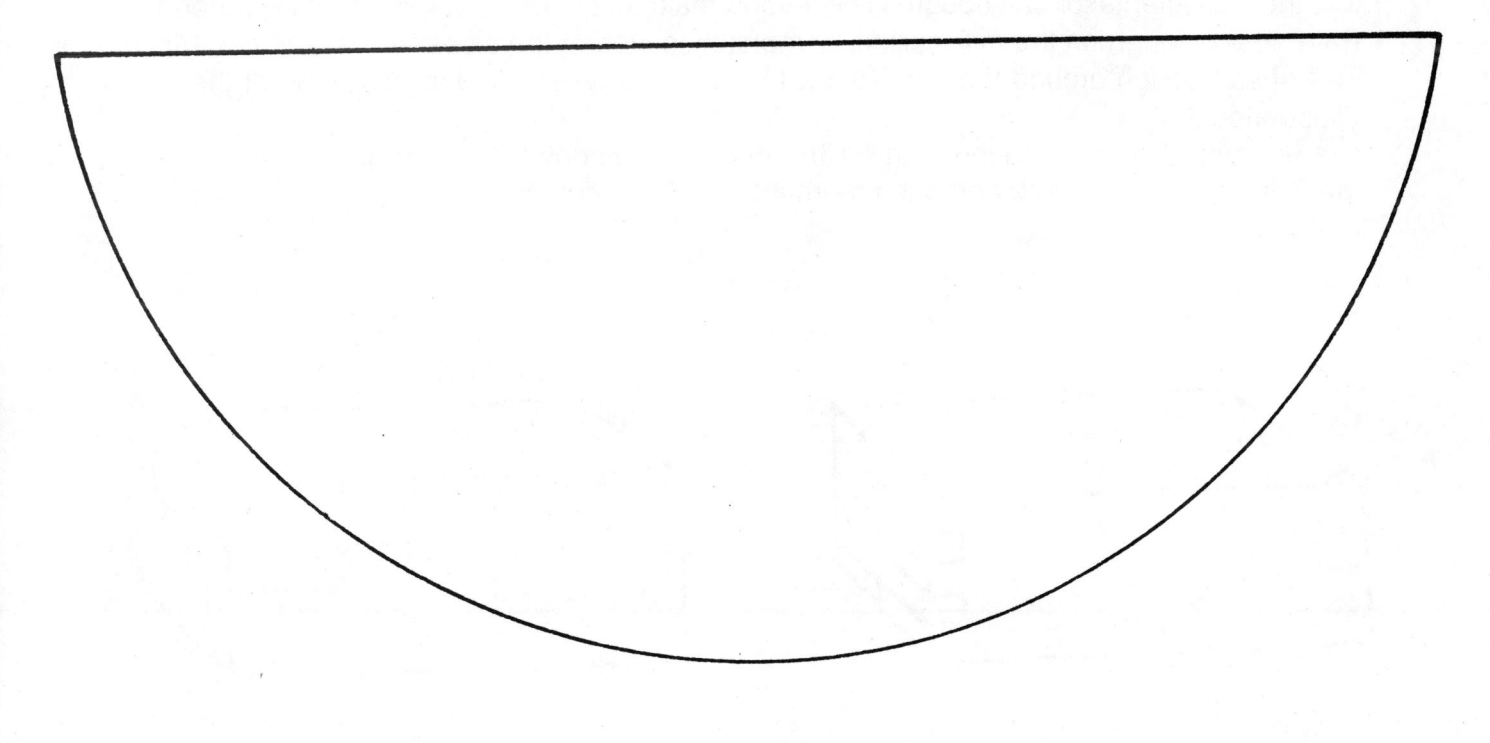

Lower face

ADDITIONAL BIBLE REFERENCES:
Abraham and Lot Go Different Ways (Genesis 13)
Jacob Steals His Brother's Blessing (Genesis 25:24-34)
Joseph Forgives His Brothers (Genesis 43:15-45:15)

BIBLE-TIME HOUSE

"Peter went up on the roof to pray." Acts 10:9b

MATERIALS:
Salt dough
Cardboard milk carton
Grocery bag
Scissors
Duct tape
Toothpick

Salt Dough Recipe
2 cups of flour
2 cups of salt
1 cup of water

INSTRUCTIONS:
1. Close the pouring spout and flatten the top of the carton. Tape in place (illustration 1).
2. Mix the ingredients for salt dough. (This recipe makes enough to cover one milk carton.)
3. Pat the salt dough on the milk carton, completely covering the sides, ends, and top. Pinch a wall of salt dough around the top. With a toothpick, draw stairs along one end of the house (illustration 2).
4. Cut rectangles from a grocery bag for the door and windows. Position the rectangles while the salt dough is still soft, and push them into it (illustration 3). The salt dough will take several days to dry.

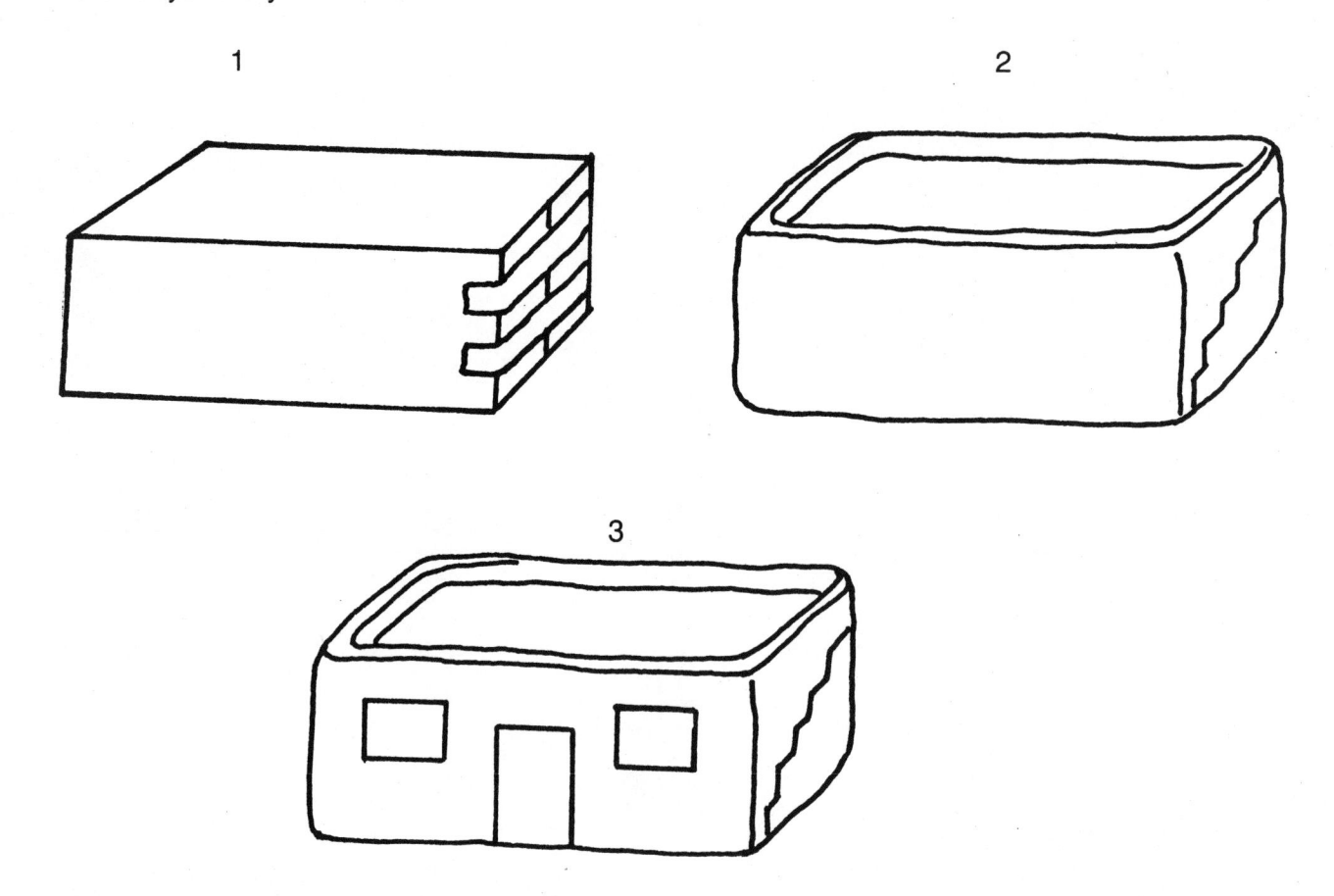

ADDITIONAL BIBLE REFERENCES:
Jesus Heals a Paralytic (Mark 2:1-12)
The Wise and Foolish Builders (Matthew 7:24-27)
Zacchaeus the Tax Collector (Luke 19:2-10)

HARP

"David would take his harp and play. Then relief would come to Saul. . . ."   1 Samuel 16:23b

MATERIALS:
Scissors or craft knife
Cardboard milk carton
5 rubber bands of varying thickness
Masking tape

INSTRUCTIONS:
1. Glue the carton closed (see page 62).
2. * Cut a hole in one side of the carton (illustration 1).
3. Stretch the rubber bands the length of the carton across the hole (illustration 2).
4. Tape the rubber bands in place on each end (illustration 3).

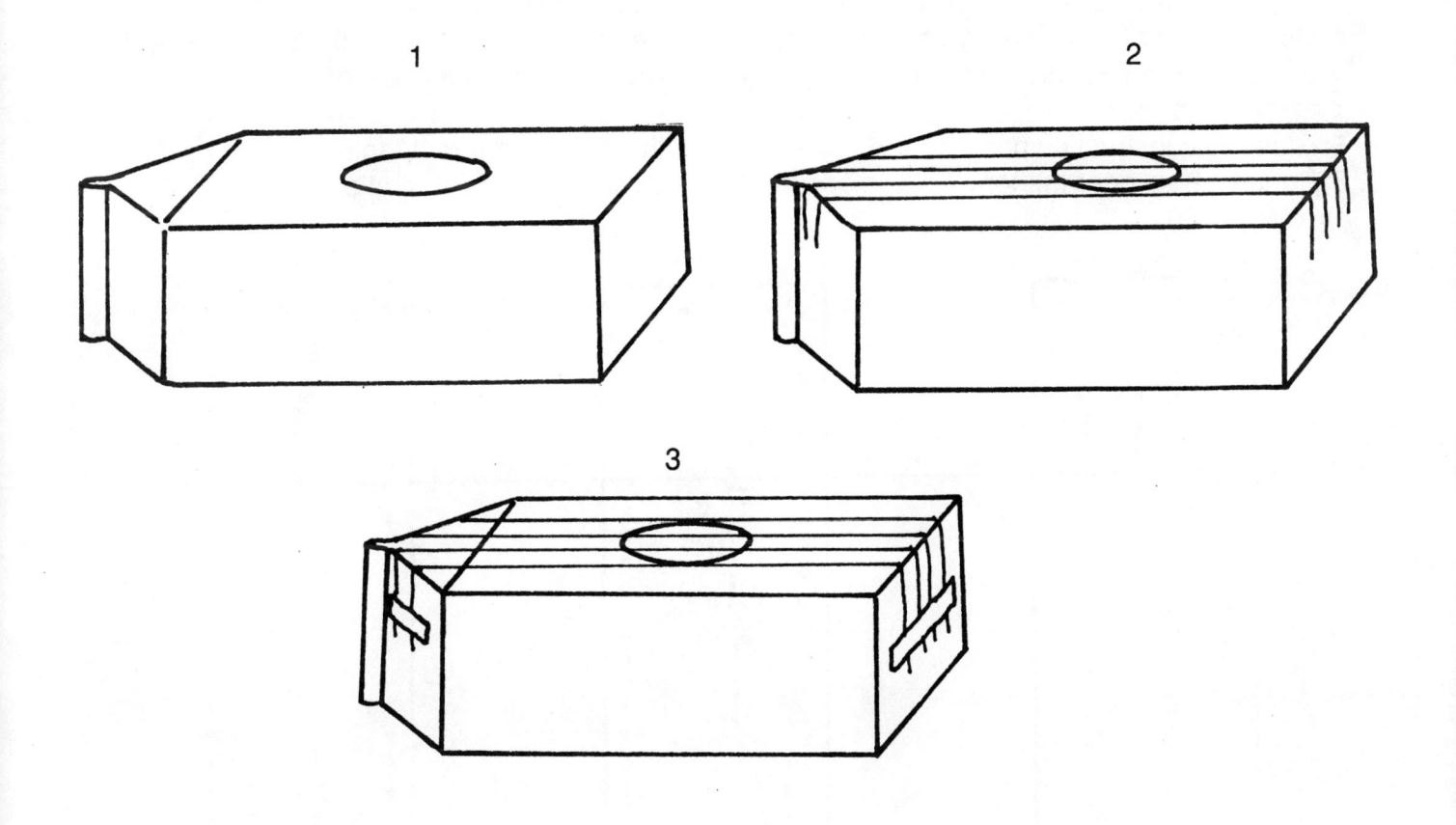

1

2

3

* To be completed by an adult.

ADDITIONAL BIBLE REFERENCES:
King Nebuchadnezzar (Daniel 3:5-7)
Praising God (Psalm 150:3-5)

BIBLE BOOKMARK

Reading God's Word and marking verses that mean a lot to us are important to a Christian's life.

MATERIALS:
Sturdy scissors
Cardboard milk carton
Construction paper
Glue
Pencil with eraser
Two stamp pads—contrasting colors
Hole punch
Yarn

INSTRUCTIONS:
1. * Cut apart the four side panels of the milk carton. Cut one panel into a rectangle 1 1/2" x 7".
2. Cut a piece of construction paper the same size.
3. Lightly print "God Is Love" vertically on the construction paper (illustration 1).
4. Use the pencil eraser as a stamp. Press the eraser on the stamp pad; then use it to print dots outlining the letters (illustration 2). Make a border around the edge of the paper with a contrasting color.
5. Glue the construction paper to the printed side of the milk carton rectangle.
6. Punch a hole near the top. Tie 6" piece of yarn through the hole (illustration 3).

* To be completed by an adult.

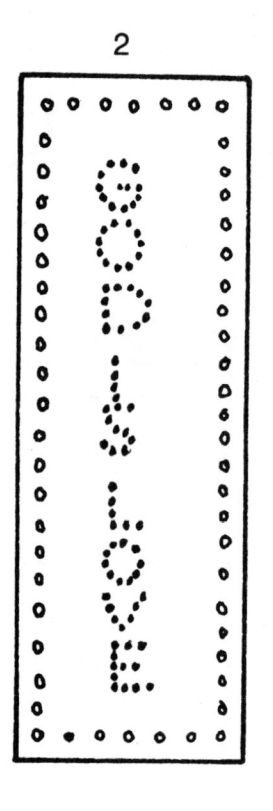

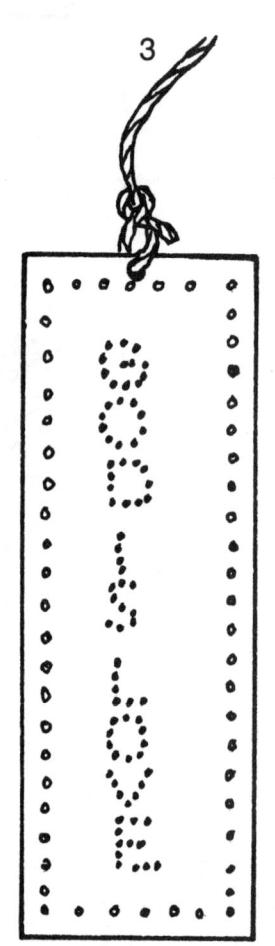

ADDITIONAL BIBLE REFERENCES:
The Bible—My Lamp (Psalm 119:105)
Memorizing God's Word (Psalm 119:11)

MAGI GIFT CONTAINER

"Then they opened their treasures and presented him with gifts . . . ."   Matthew 2:11b

MATERIALS:
Sturdy scissors or craft knife
Cardboard milk carton
Glue
Construction paper
Magi patterns, page 76
Markers
Glitter and trim
Large, gold self-adhesive circle
Glue

INSTRUCTIONS:
1. Glue the pouring spout of the carton closed.
2. * Make a cut on three sides of the carton 5" from the bottom. Leave the fourth side intact (illustration 1).
3. Glue construction paper to the upper and lower portions of the milk carton.
4. Using the patterns on page 76, cut two face rectangles from pink, tan, or brown construction paper. Glue a rectangle on each side of the angled top of the carton. Trace facial features on one side. Cut two triangles from the same colored paper to cover the ends (illustration 2).
5. Using the pattern, cut a crown from gold construction paper, and glue it on top of the carton.
6. Add glitter and trim to the front to look like rich robes and jewels.
7. Make arms from two strips of 1" x 6" construction paper. Glue one to each side of the carton. Angle the arms so they cross in front. A small gift may be placed inside the carton. Close the top and seal it with a gold self-adhesive circle (illustration 3).

1   2 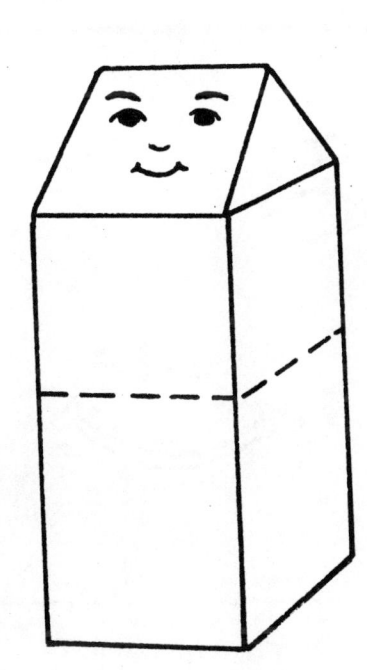   3

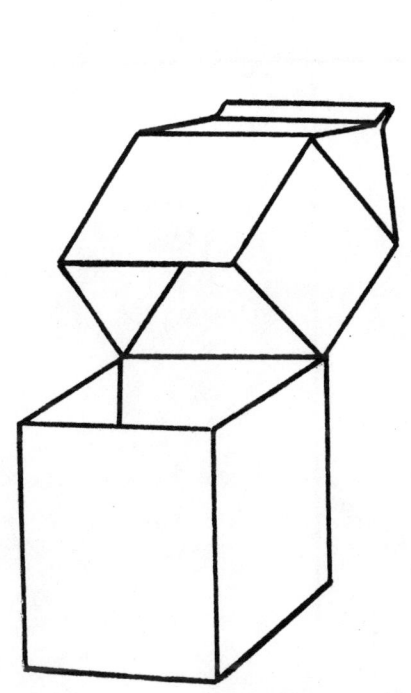

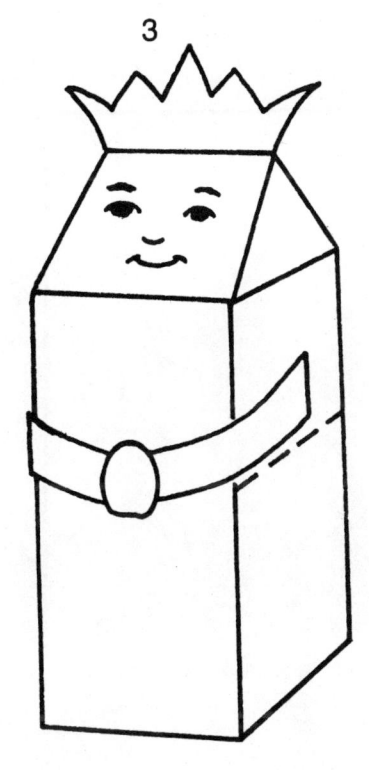

* To be completed by an adult.

Shining Star Publications, Copyright © 1994   SS3805

MAGI PATTERNS

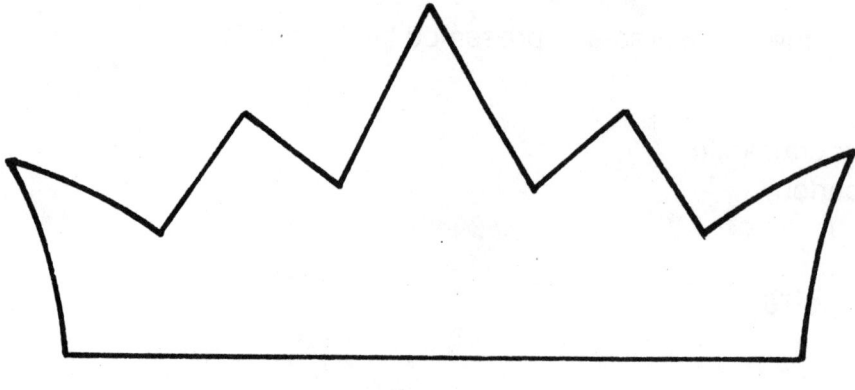

Crown

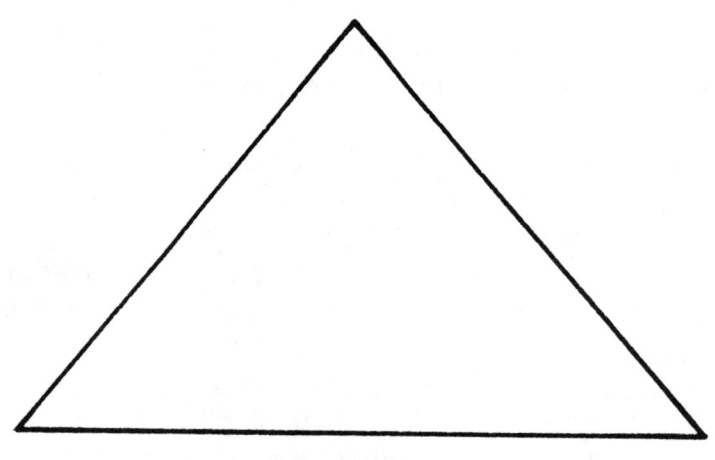

Triangle end
(Cut two)

Face rectangle
(Cut two)

STAR LUMINARY

"When they saw the star, they were overjoyed."

Matthew 2:10

MATERIALS:
Sturdy scissors
Spray paint
Cardboard milk carton
Star pattern, page 88
Pencil
Sand
Votive candle
Nail

INSTRUCTIONS:
1. * Cut the top off the carton (illustration 1).
2. Trace the star pattern on page 88 on one side of the carton (illustration 2).
3. * Use the nail to punch holes at regular intervals outlining the star (illustration 3). Use a pencil to make the holes larger, if necessary.
4. * The carton may be spray painted, if desired.
5. Put about an inch of sand in the bottom of the carton. Place a votive candle in it. * Light the candle and place it outside. Line a walk with several of these luminaries.

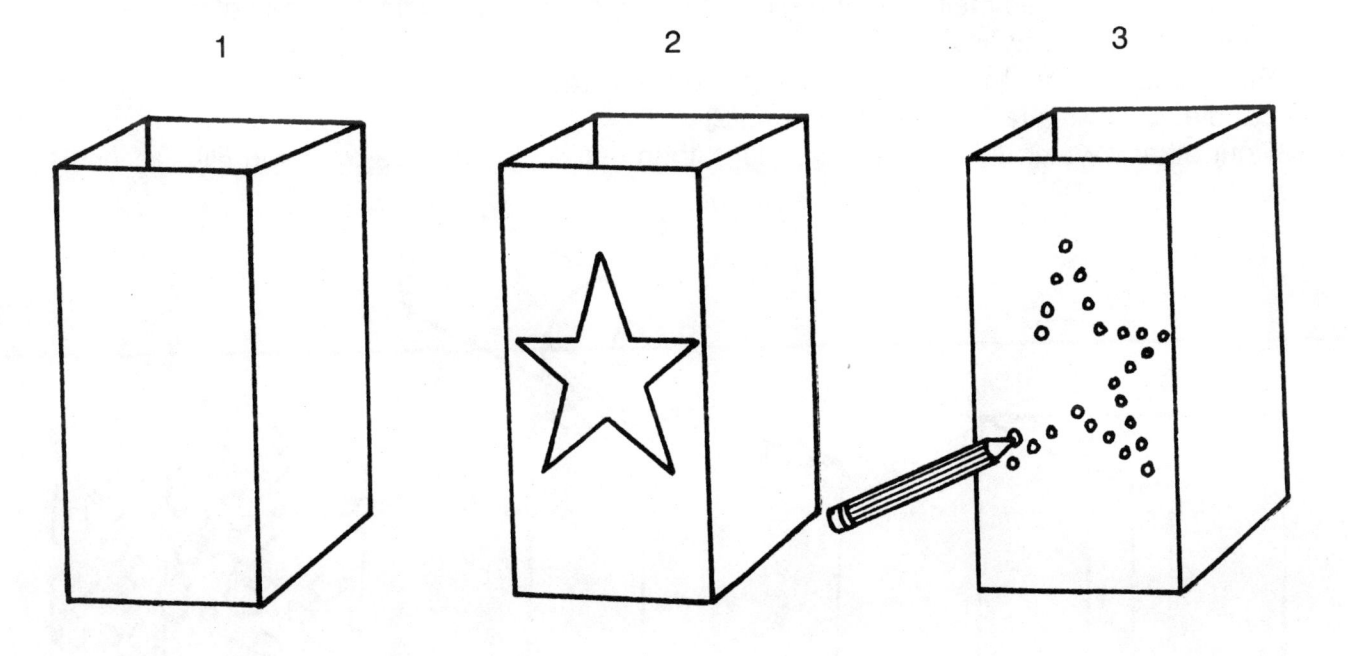

1   2   3

* To be completed by an adult.

LACY CANDLE

"The people living in darkness have seen a great light."   Matthew 4:16a

MATERIALS:
Sturdy scissors
Hot plate or stove
Cardboard milk carton
Cracked ice
Candle
Paraffin
Pan and tin can
Water
Pot holders
Old crayons (optional)

INSTRUCTIONS:
1. * Cut the top off the carton. Make the carton as tall as the candle you are using. Put a little melted paraffin in the middle of the carton and hold the candle in place until the paraffin hardens (illustration 1).
2. * Carefully melt enough paraffin to fill the carton mold. Place the paraffin in a can, in a pan of water. Never put the container with paraffin directly on the heat. Watch the paraffin constantly. When it has melted, use pot holders to pick it up. Paraffin may be colored by adding shavings of old crayons.
3. Fill the carton mold with cracked ice. * Pour the melted paraffin over the ice and standing candle. Let the paraffin cool (illustration 2).
4. Pour off any water. Allow to dry overnight; then tear off the milk carton mold (illustration 3).

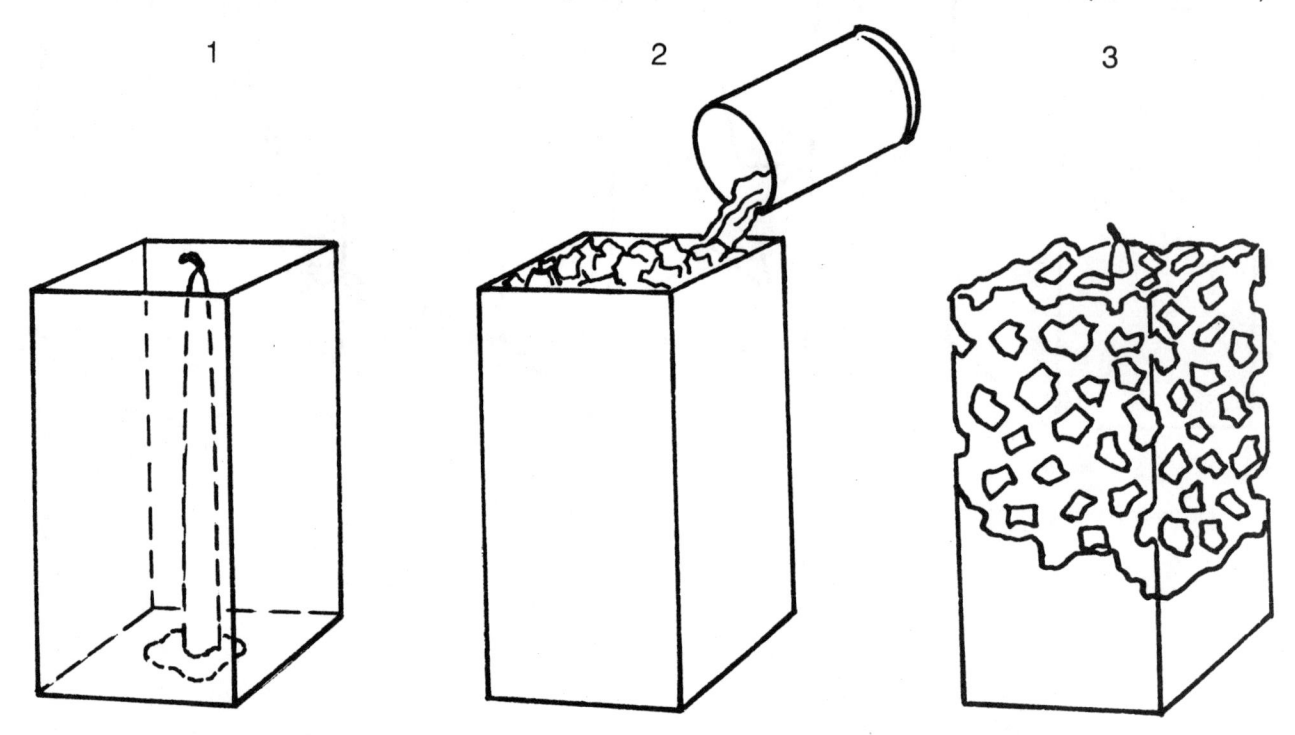

* To be completed by an adult.

EASTER PLANTER

"[They] put him to death by nailing him to the cross." Acts 2:23b

MATERIALS:
Sturdy scissors or craft knife
Cardboard milk carton
Cross pattern, page 80
Potting soil
Flowering plant
Decoration (see page 6)
Pencil

INSTRUCTIONS:
1. * Cut off the top of the carton (illustration 1).
2. * Cut away three sides of the carton leaving a 3 1/2" base to hold the plant (illustration 2).
3. * Use the pattern on page 80 to cut a cross in the remaining side (illustration 3). This will be the back of the planter.
4. Decorate the planter with one of the ideas on page 6.
5. Put potting soil in the base and plant a flower.

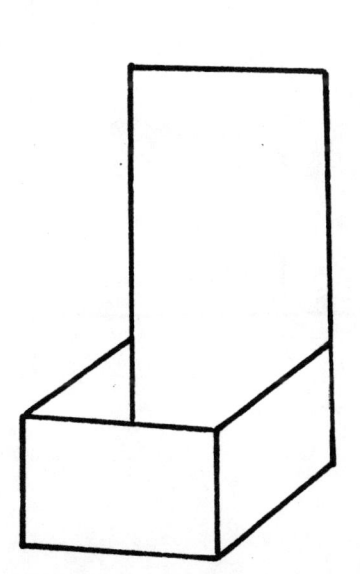

1   2   3

* To be completed by an adult.

CROSS PATTERN

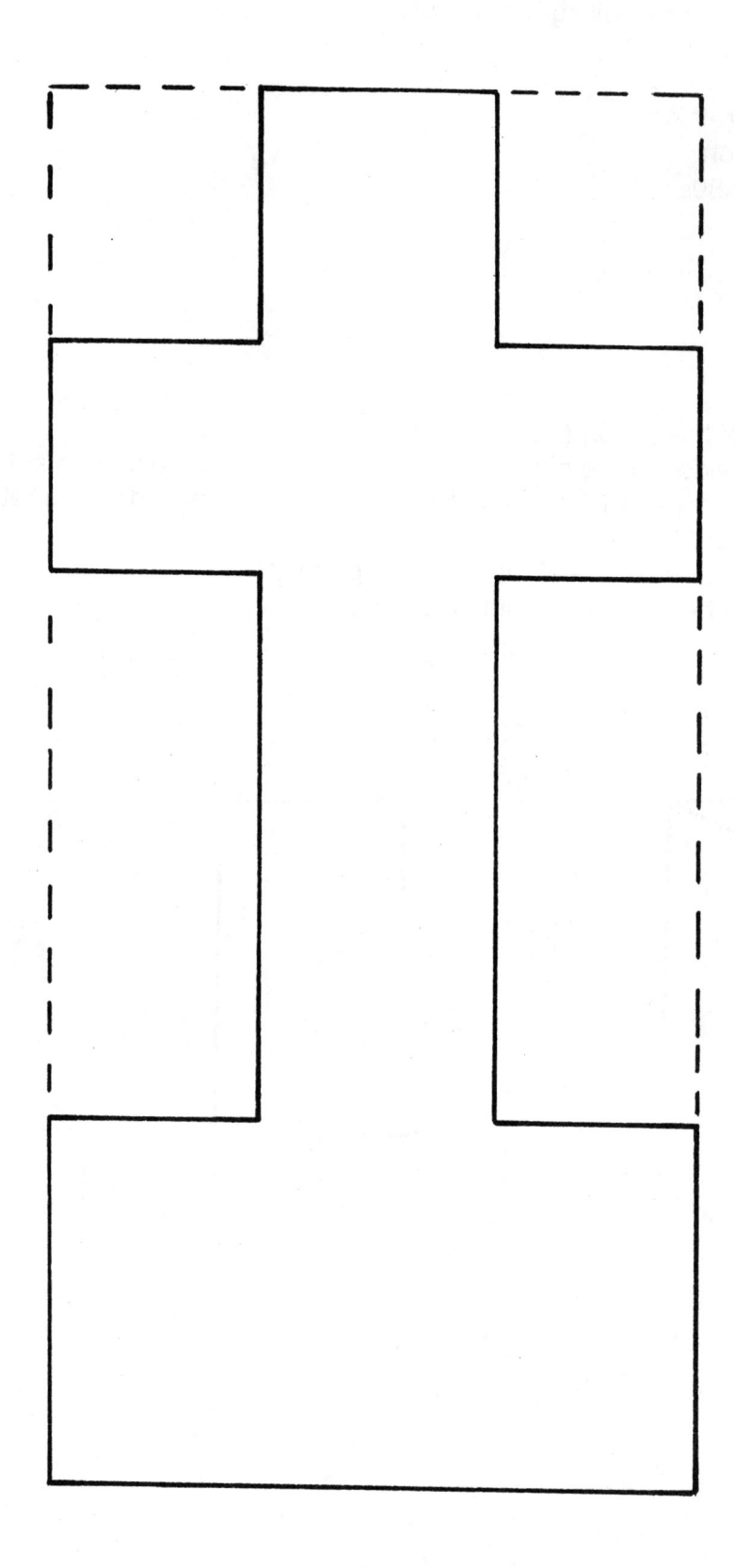

CRAFT IDEAS USING EGG CARTONS

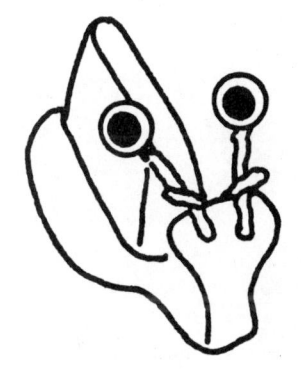

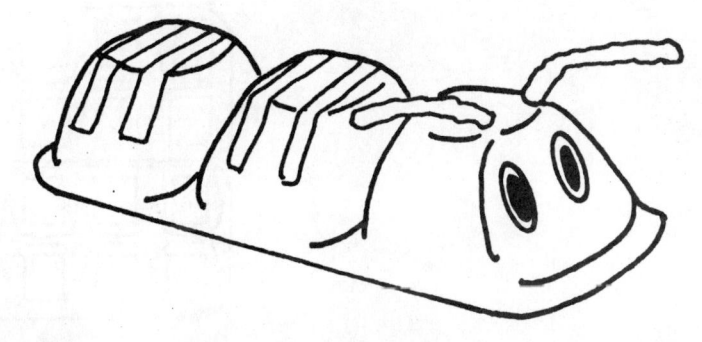

ADVENT CALENDAR

The countdown to Christmas can be a time for daily devotions. Inside each section of this Advent calendar is a Bible verse for children to read.

MATERIALS:
2 egg cartons
Stapler
Glue
Clip-type clothespins
Bible verse references, page 83
Scissors
Old Christmas cards
Heading pattern, page 84
Tagboard
Pencil
Glitter (optional)
Markers or crayons

INSTRUCTIONS:
1. Cut the lids from both egg cartons. Save one lid for another project. Staple the two egg carton bottom halves together, long side to long side (illustration 1).
2. Reproduce the Bible verse references on page 83. Cut them into strips and fold accordion-style. Place a dab of glue on the end of each strip of paper, and place a verse inside each egg carton section. Keep the verses in order.
3. Cut twenty-four 1 3/4" squares from old Christmas cards. (Make a 1 3/4" square from tagboard to use as a pattern.) Glue a flap over each egg carton section (illustration 2).
4. Glue one lid to the top edge of the cartons with the flat side up (illustration 3). Reproduce the heading pattern from page 84. Color it, and add glitter if desired. Cut it out and glue it to the lid.

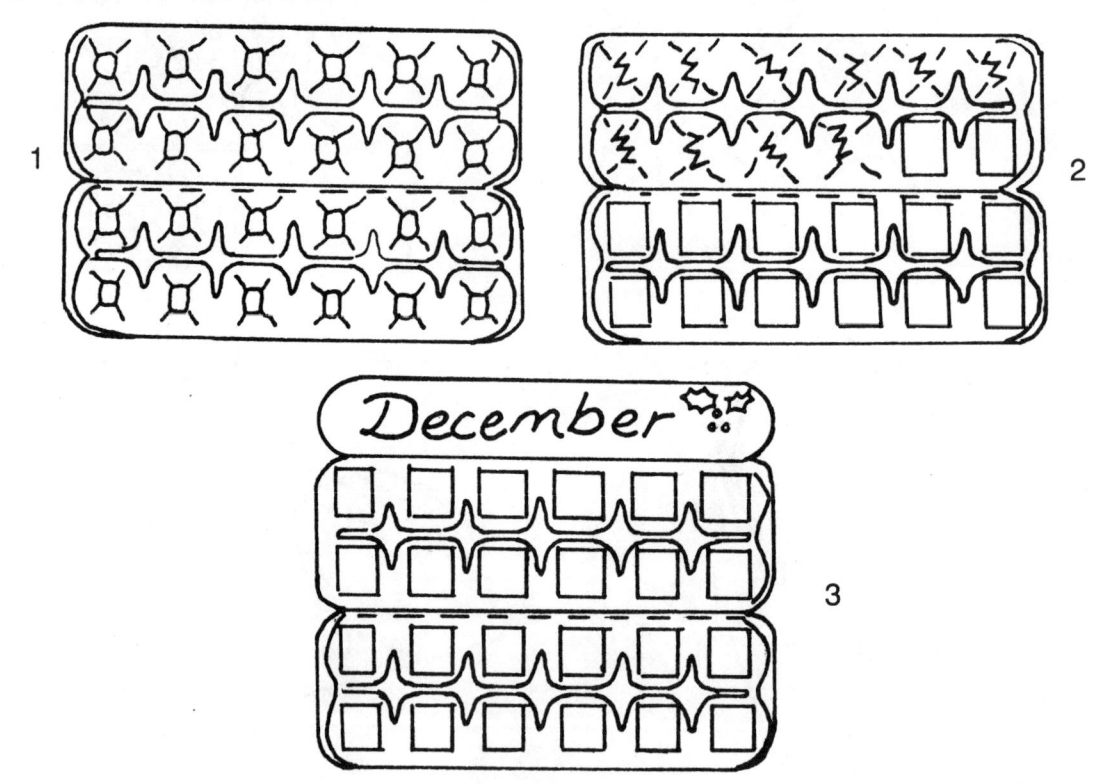

ADVENT BIBLE VERSES

1. John 1:1

2. Isaiah 7:14

3. Luke 1:26-28

4. Luke 1:30-31

5. Luke 1:42

6. Matthew 1:20-21

7. Matthew 1:22-23

8. Luke 1:32-34

9. Matthew 24:42

10. Micah 5:2

11. Luke 2:1,3

12. Luke 2:4-5

13. John 1:9

14. Luke 2:6-7

15. Isaiah 9:6

16. Luke 2:8-10

17. Luke 2:11-12

18. Luke 2:16-17

19. Matthew 2:1-2

20. Matthew 2:9-11

21. John 1:14

22. John 13:34

23. John 18:37

24. Luke 2:14

ADVENT CALENDAR HEADING

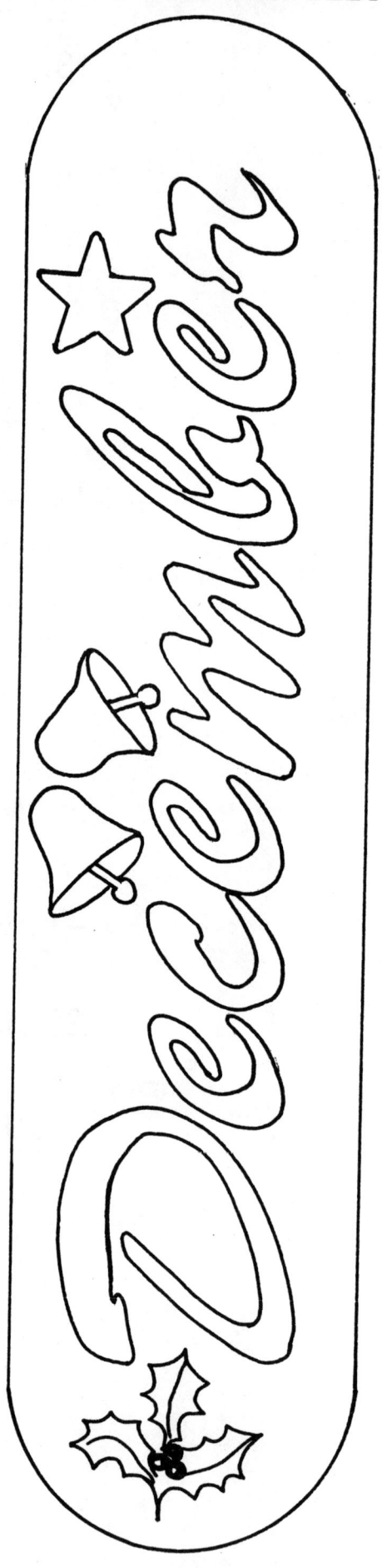

CREATURES THAT MOVE ON THE GROUND

"Rule over . . . every living creature that moves on the ground."   Genesis 1:28b

MATERIALS:
Egg cartons
Scissors
Black pipe cleaners
Wiggle eyes
Construction paper
Glue

SPIDER

INSTRUCTIONS:
1. Cut the egg carton into individual sections. Trim the edges.
2. Turn a section upside down. Force eight 3" black pipe cleaners through opposite sides for legs. Bend a short piece inside the cup to hold it in place. Make an L-shaped bend in each leg.
3. Glue wiggle eyes on one side (illustration 1).

CATERPILLAR

INSTRUCTIONS:
1. Cut the egg carton into three-cup sections.
2. Turn it upside down. Add antennae by forcing two 3" pipe cleaners through the top of one end section (illustration 2). Bend ends inside the cup to hold in place.
3. Glue two wiggle eyes to the face on the front section.
4. Add construction paper stripes, if desired.

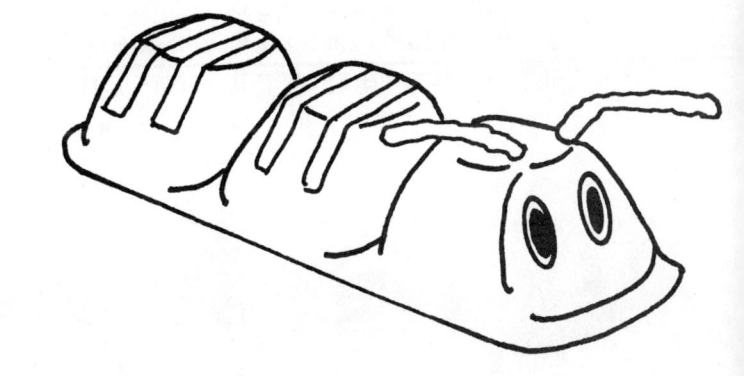

SNAIL

INSTRUCTIONS:
1. Cut out one section from the bottom of an egg carton, and turn it upside down onto the lid. Trace around the hump to form a snail's head. Cut out, and glue hump to the snail's body (illustration 1).
2. Force a 1 3/4" piece of pipe cleaner through each side near the top of the head for antennae (illustration 2). Twist the short end around the pipe cleaner to hold it in place.
3. Glue a wiggle eye to the end of each pipe cleaner (illustration 3).

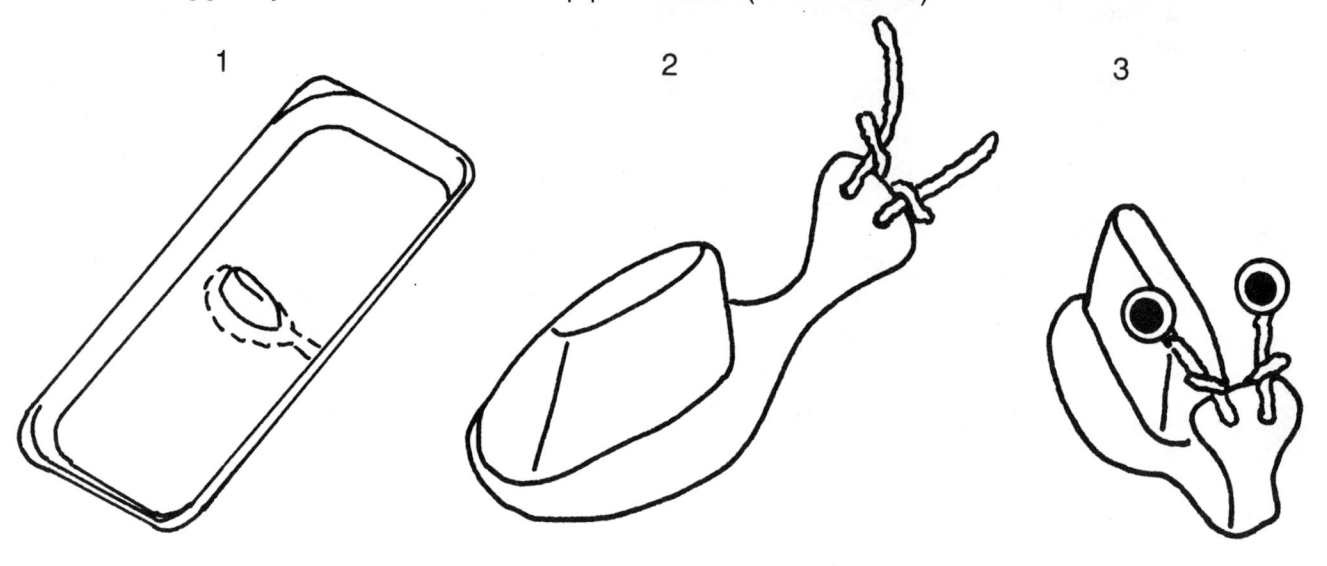

1   2   3

BEETLE

INSTRUCTIONS:
1. Cut apart an individual and a corner section from an egg carton (illustration 1). Cut away the irregular portion from the corner section, leaving only the bottom and two curved sides.
2. Glue the corner section to the front of the individual section (illustration 2).
3. Add six pipe cleaners for legs: Two 2" legs near the rear and two 1 3/4" legs near the midpoint. Bend all four legs back. Force two 1 3/4" pipe cleaner legs in the sides of the front section. Bend back all the ends inside the carton so they will stay in place (illustration 3).
4. Glue two wiggle eyes to the front (corner) section.

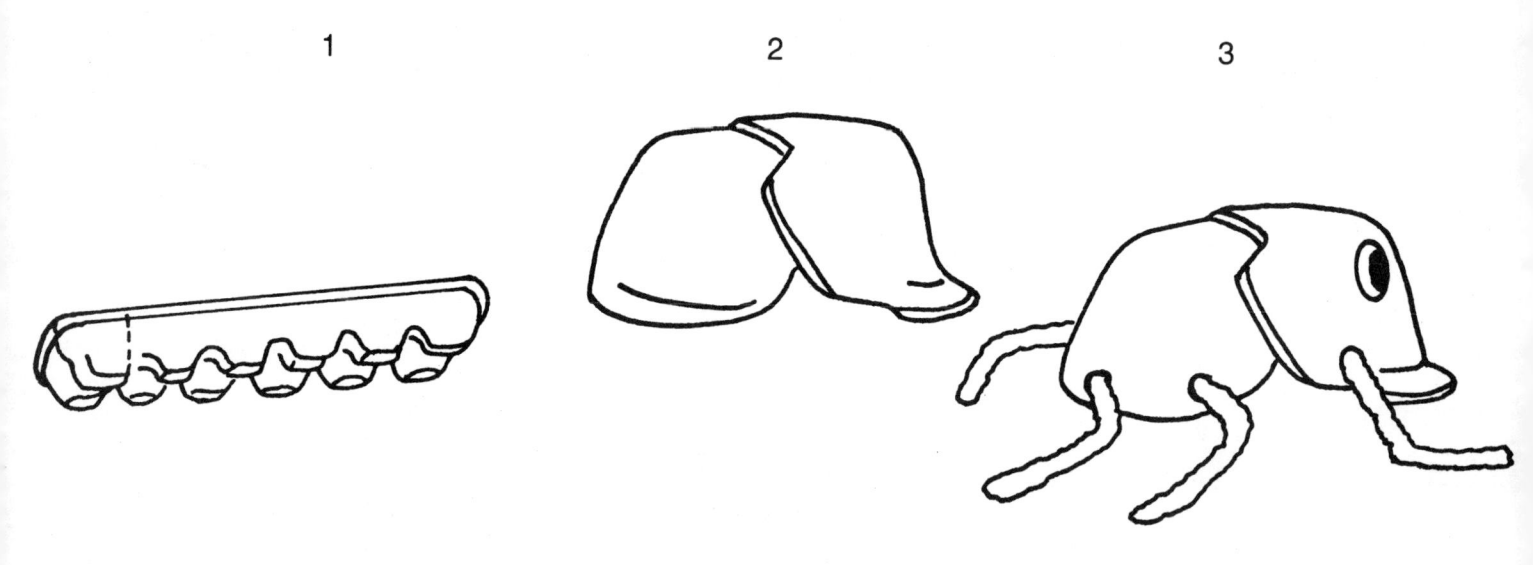

1   2   3

LILIES OF THE FIELD

". . . See how the lilies of the field grow." Matthew 6:28a

MATERIALS:
Egg carton
Scissors
Pipe cleaners
Leaf patterns, page 88
Flower base pattern, page 88
3 toilet paper tubes
Paint and paintbrush
Yarn or ribbon
Construction paper
Glue

INSTRUCTIONS:
1. Cut $1/2$" off one toilet paper tube and 1" off a second tube. Paint all three tubes; then allow them to dry.
2. Cut the egg carton into individual sections. Shape each section into flower petals by cutting out long triangle shapes at the four corners. Round the tops (illustration 1). You may want to save the scraps to make the "Love Mosaic" on page 89.
3. Using the flower base pattern on page 88, cut this shape from construction paper. Glue the egg carton petals to the center of the construction paper flower base. Allow it to dry.
4. Using the leaf patterns on page 88, cut leaves from green construction paper. Glue two to a pipe cleaner. Allow them to dry.
5. Assemble the vase by standing the three painted tubes together. Tie them with a length of yarn or ribbon (illustration 2).
6. Force the pipe cleaner through the center of the flower. Bend the short end to hold in place (illustration 3). Make several flowers, and put them in the vase.

1   2    3

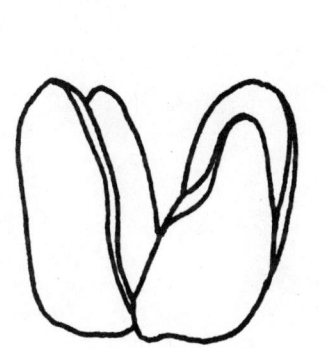

ADDITIONAL BIBLE REFERENCE:
Creation (Genesis 1-2)

LILY PATTERNS

Leaves

Flower base

STAR LUMINARY PATTERN

THE GOSPEL IN ONE WORD IS LOVE

"Be devoted to one another in brotherly love." Romans 12:10a

MATERIALS:
Sharp scissors
Polystyrene egg cartons in various colors
Rectangular polystyrene tray
Love pattern, page 90
Pencil
Glue
Yarn
Hole punch

INSTRUCTIONS:
1. * Cut the egg cartons into small, irregularly shaped pieces.
2. Reproduce the love pattern on page 90, and place it in the center of the polystyrene tray. Firmly trace the letters, leaving an imprint in the tray (illustration 1).
3. Glue the egg carton pieces inside the letters traced on the tray (illustration 2).
4. To create a hanger, punch two holes near the top of the tray. Run a 12" piece of yarn through the holes, and tie the ends together (illustration 3).

1　　　　　　　　2　　　　　　　　3

* To be completed by an adult.

ADDITIONAL BIBLE REFERENCES:
Loving God (Matthew 22:37)
Loving Others (Mark 12:31a)
What Is Love? (1 Corinthians 13:4a)

LOVE PATTERN

CROSS

"He humbled himself and became obedient to death—even death on a cross!"

Philippians 2:8b

MATERIALS:
2 egg cartons
3" squares of colored tissue paper
Glue
String
Heavy-duty needle
Scissors

INSTRUCTIONS:
1. Cut the lid off both egg cartons and save for another project.
2. Form a cross with the two bottom sections (illustration 1).
3. Stitch the two egg cartons together in the center, and tie a knot in the back (illustration 2).
4. Lightly crumple individual squares of tissue paper. Glue one inside each egg carton section (illustration 3). Use a variety of brightly colored tissue paper squares.

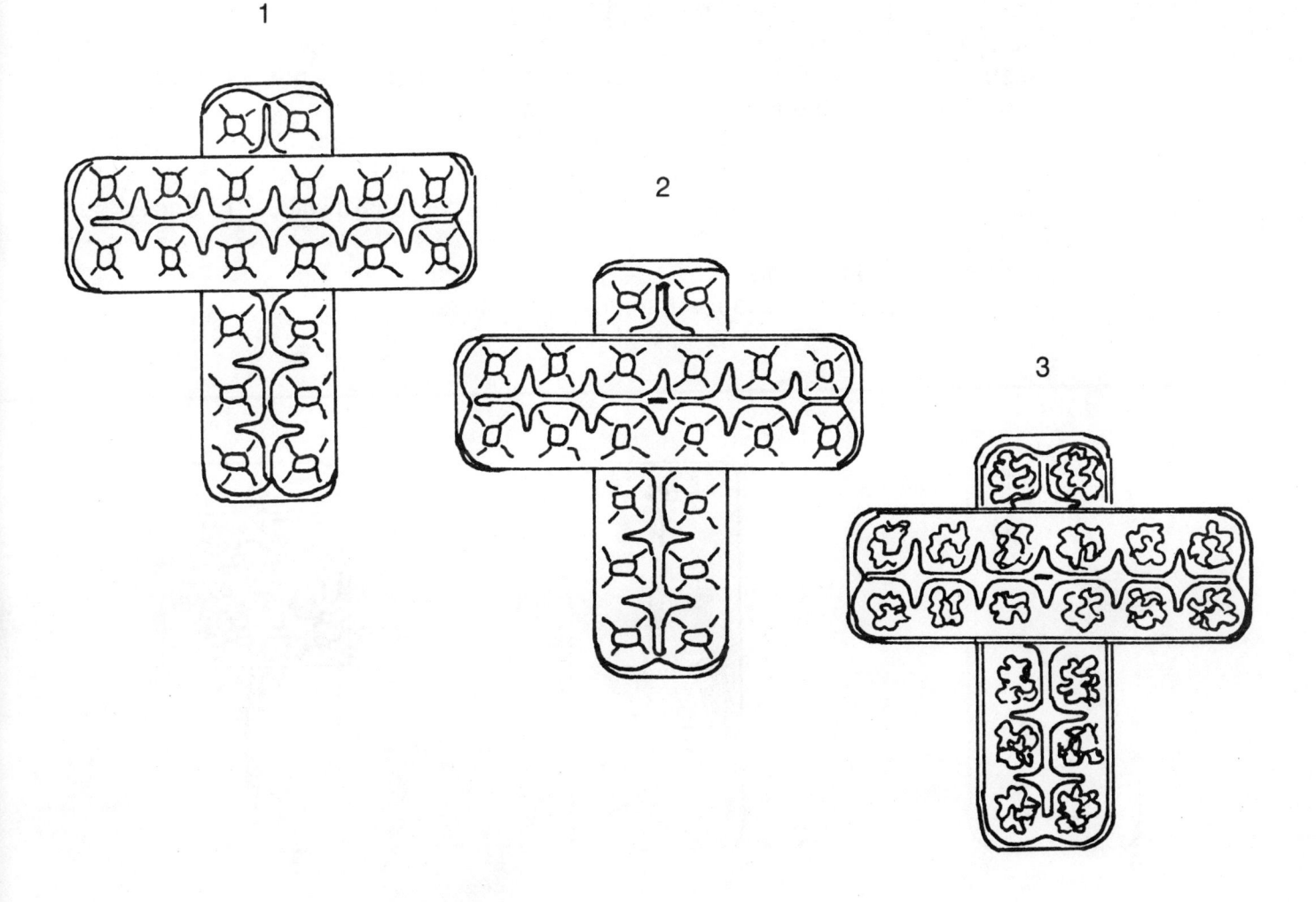

ADDITIONAL BIBLE REFERENCES:
Following Jesus (Matthew 10:38; 16:24)
Jesus' Cross (Matthew 27:32)

JESUS' ASCENSION

"He was taken up before their very eyes, and a cloud hid him from their sight." Acts 1:9b

MATERIALS:
Egg carton lid
Scissors
Blue construction paper
Glue
Yarn
Jesus pattern on this page
Tape
Manila folder or lightweight cardboard
Cotton balls
Hole punch

Jesus Pattern

INSTRUCTIONS:
1. Cut the egg carton lid from the base. Save the base for another project.
2. Glue blue construction paper to the face of the lid, covering the sides and ends. Punch a hole approximately 1 1/2" from each end of the lid (illustration 1).
3. String yarn through the two holes. Tie the two ends together on the inside of the lid. Tape the figure of Jesus on the yarn. Position the figure so that the knot does not prevent the figure from moving up and down the face of the lid (illustration 2).
4. Cut the manila folder or cardboard into a 6" square. Make a 1 1/2" fold along two parallel sides. (The cardboard will fold easily if you score the fold line with a scissors blade first.) Glue the folded edges to the sides of the egg carton lid. The cardboard will be 1/2" above the lid (illustration 3).
5. Cover the cardboard with cotton balls.
6. Move the figure of Jesus so that it disappears under the clouds.

1   2    3

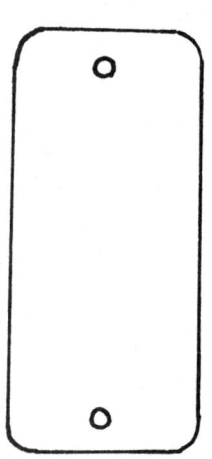

Shining Star Publications, Copyright © 1994   SS3805

Dear Family,

Several of our craft projects this year use recycled materials. We need your help collecting a number of items. Listed below are the materials we would like for you to save. Make sure each item is clean. Take special care with polystyrene trays that have held meat and poultry. These trays need to be scrubbed in hot sudsy water.

Please save the following:

- 12-ounce frozen juice cans and lids
- Cardboard tubes from toilet paper, paper towels, and gift wrap
- Brown paper grocery bags
- Polystyrene (Styrofoam™) trays
- Half-gallon cardboard milk and juice cartons
- Egg cartons

Thank you for your help!

Your child's teacher

INDEX
BIBLE STORIES

Creation 8, 29, 31, 32, 55, 85, 86, 87	Angel Appears to Zechariah 15
The Serpent Tempts Eve 31	Christmas Story 17, 18, 19, 37, 45, 60, 77, 82
Noah's Ark...29	King Herod 47
Tower of Babel 35, 42	Visit of the Magi........................14, 19, 75
Abraham and Lot Go Different Ways 71	Calling the First Disciples.......................67
Abraham's Visitors 14	Jesus, the Light of the World.............26, 78
Lot's Wife 35	Feeding the Multitude 48
Jacob Steals His Brother's Blessing 71	Jesus Walks on Water...........................67
Jacob's Ladder...............................15, 42	Jesus the Good Shepherd 30
Joseph Sold as a Slave 35	Zacchaeus the Tax Collector...................72
Joseph Forgives His Brothers..................71	The Wise and Foolish Builders 72
Moses and Aaron Go to Pharaoh 14	Woman Touches Jesus' Cloak 46
Crossing the Red Sea......................16, 35	The Faith of the Centurion 33
Moses' Hands Grow Tired......................42	Jesus Blesses the Children.....................53
Moses at Mt. Sinai 13	Jesus Calms the Storm..........................67
Ten Commandments..............................43	Jesus Heals a Paralytic..........................72
Balaam and His Donkey 15, 30	Jesus' Triumphant Entry 30, 38
Crossing into the Promised Land..............42	Parable of the Sower 8
Battle of Jericho 13, 42	The Prodigal Son 46
Gideon 15	The Resurrection 15, 22, 23, 39, 79
Samson..29	The Resurrected Christ..........................48
Samuel's Robe.....................................46	Jesus' Ascension 91, 92
King David.....................................47, 73	Showing Love 49, 58, 89
Solomon's Riches 16	God's Word 28, 57, 74
Solomon's Wise Ruling 14	Praising God..9, 10, 11, 12, 13, 36, 59, 63, 73
Elijah Goes to Heaven 16	Pentecost 50
Queen Esther 47	Peter's Rescue.....................................15
Mordecai Honored 46	Philip and the Ethiopian 16
King Nebuchadnezzar..................14, 47, 73	Paul Credits God for Seasons 55
Daniel Praises God 55, 69	Paul Talks About Death......................24, 47
Daniel in the Lions' Den 30	Prayer 25, 65
Jonah 48	Trust 52

BIBLE REFERENCES

Reference	Page
Genesis 1-2	8, 26, 32, 48, 55, 85, 87
Genesis 3:1a	31
Genesis 6:20	29
Genesis 11:1-9	35, 42
Genesis 13	71
Genesis 18	14
Genesis 19:26	35
Genesis 25:24-34	71
Genesis 28:10-22	15, 42
Genesis 37:3-36	35, 46
Genesis 43:15-45:15	71
Exodus 5:1-12	14
Exodus 7:12	31
Exodus 13:17-14:31	35
Exodus 14	16
Exodus 17:8-16	28, 42
Exodus 19	13
Exodus 34:28b	43
Numbers 22:21-35	15, 30
Deuteronomy 6:5	58
Deuteronomy 30:14	57
Joshua 4:3a	42
Joshua 6	13, 42
Joshua 24:15b	63
Judges 5:12b	12
Judges 6:1-16	15
Judges 14:5-18	30
1 Samuel 2:18-19	46
1 Samuel 16:23b	73
2 Samuel 5:1-5	47
2 Samuel 22:29	26
1 Kings 3:16-28	14
1 Kings 10:23-29	16
2 Kings 2:11-12	16
2 Kings 21:1-23:25	28
1 Chronicles 16:34	36
1 Chronicles 29:13	36
2 Chronicles 33:1-35:27	28
Esther 2:1-18	47
Esther 6	46
Psalm 18:28	26
Psalm 39:12a	65
Psalm 45:17a	66
Psalm 81:1-3	13
Psalm 95:2a	36
Psalm 100:1	10
Psalm 119:11	74
Psalm 119:105	74
Psalm 150:3-5	9, 73
Psalm 150:5	11
Proverbs 3:1	57
Ecclesiastes 3:1	55
Isaiah 40:31	52
Jeremiah 36	28
Daniel 2:20-23	55
Daniel 3	14, 47, 73
Daniel 6	30, 69
Jonah 1:17	48
Matthew 2:1-12	14, 19, 47, 75, 77
Matthew 4:16a	78
Matthew 6:6a	63
Matthew 6:28a	87
Matthew 7:7	63
Matthew 7:24-27	72
Matthew 8:5	33
Matthew 8:18-27	50, 67
Matthew 10:16b	31
Matthew 10:38; 16:24	91
Matthew 14:13-21	48
Matthew 22:37	89
Matthew 27:32	91
Matthew 27:45-54	33
Matthew 28:1-7	15
Mark 1:16-19	67
Mark 2:1-12	72
Mark 6:45-51	67
Mark 11:1-11	30
Mark 12:31a	89
Luke 1:5-25	15
Luke 1:26-38	15
Luke 2:7b	45
Luke 2:9a	18

Luke 2:16	19
Luke 4:17a	28
Luke 5:6b	48
Luke 8:4-15	8
Luke 11:1-4	65
Luke 15:20-24	46
Luke 18:16b	53
Luke 19:2-10	72
Luke 24:2-3	22
Luke 24:36-44	48
John 1:3a	32
John 1:5a	26
John 3:7-8	50
John 10:11-16	30
John 12:13a	38
John 13:35	49
John 14:15	58
John 15:17	58
John 21:6	67
Acts 1:9b	92
Acts 2:2a, 23b	50, 79
Acts 8:30a	16
Acts 10	33
Acts 10:9b	72
Acts 12:3-10	15
Acts 14:15b-17	55
Acts 14:17	25
Acts 23:12-35	33
Romans 12:10a	89
1 Corinthians 9:25b	47
1 Corinthians 13:4a	89
Ephesians 5:20	25
Philippians 2:8b	91
Philippians 4:6	65
1 Thessalonians 5:16-18	25
1 Timothy 4:4	8, 36
Hebrews 12:28	59
Revelation 3:20a	63

HOLIDAY CRAFTS

Thanksgiving
    Napkin Rings 36
    Wall Hanging 59

Christmas
    Advent Calendar 82
    Advent Candles 37
    Angel 18
    Christmas Ornament 17
    Lacy Candle 78
    Magi Gift Container 75
    Nativity Set 19
    Stable 45
    Star Luminary 77
    Star of David 60

Easter
    Angel 18
    Butterfly 39
    Cross 91
    Easter Planter 79
    Empty Tomb 22
    Jesus' Ascension 92
    Mini Easter Basket 23
    Palm Branch 38